DAILY

MEDITERRANEAN DIET

Cookbook for Beginners 2023

1800 Quick Delicious Recipes for Your Whole Famliy, 28-Days Meal Plan to Build New, Healthy Habits

Natasha Pollard

CONTENTS

Poultry And Meats Recipes 17

Fish And Seafood Recipes 28

Vegetable Mains And Meatless Recipes 39

Sides , Salads, And Soups Recipes 50

Beans , Grains, And Pastas Recipes 62

INTRODUCTION

Natasha Pollard's Introduction to Tasting Drugs: A Culinary Journey

Enter the world of Natasha Pollard's Mediterranean Diet Cookbook - a tribute to the culinary expertise of the region. The allure of the Mediterranean goes beyond its crystal-clear waters and sun-drenched shores. A region where food tells a story, centuries of tradition condensed in every bite, where health and flavor dance in harmonious delight.

Natasha's love of the Mediterranean is not just about its dishes, but the stories behind them. From the bustling markets of Spain to the serene olive groves of Greece, she curates recipes that are both authentic and innovative. Every page you turn is not just a recipe; it's a recipe. It is the gateway to the Mediterranean haven.

Through travel, Natasha discovered that the Mediterranean diet is not just a diet, but a way of life. A lifestyle that combines taste and wellness, tradition and innovation, simplicity and abundance. It's a testament to the region's philosophy: the best things in life are often the simplest.

In this cookbook, Natasha doesn't just share recipes, she shares recipes. She invites you into her world. A world where food is more than just sustenance; it's an experience, a memory, a joyful celebration of life. So let Natasha be your guide as you embark on a culinary journey through the Mediterranean. Through her eyes, you will savor, savor and enjoy every moment of this delicious journey.

About the Mediterranean Diet

The Mediterranean Diet, rooted in the traditional eating habits of the people living around the Mediterranean Sea, is much more than a mere diet plan; it's a lifestyle. This dietary pattern emphasizes fresh fruits and vegetables, whole grains, legumes, nuts, and olive oil, making it rich in fiber and antioxidants. It encourages moderate consumption of lean proteins like fish and poultry, and minimal intake of red meat. Wine, especially red, is enjoyed in moderation.

This diet isn't just about food, but also about enjoying meals with family and friends, and coupling it with regular physical activity, thereby promoting overall well-being. Studies have shown that it can lead to weight loss, improve heart health, and may even help prevent chronic conditions like diabetes and certain types of cancer.

Perhaps the most appealing part of the Mediterranean Diet is its accessibility and sustainability. The focus isn't on restriction, but on nourishment and pleasure, and with a wealth of flavors and ingredients to choose from, it's a diet that can easily be maintained for a lifetime. So, adopting the Mediterranean Diet isn't just about eating better; it's about living better.

Characteristics of the Mediterranean diet

Primary Fat Source - Olive Oil

The diet mainly relies on olive oil as the chief source of added fat. Olive oil, especially extra virgin, is rich in monounsaturated fats and antioxidants. Its consumption is linked to reduced oxidative stress and inflammation.

Plant-Based Food

A large portion of the diet consists of fresh vegetables, fruits, legumes, nuts, and whole grains. These are rich in essential vitamins, minerals, fiber, and phytonutrients.

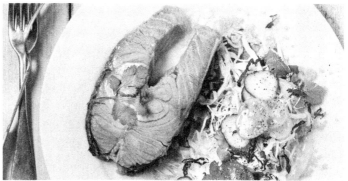

Fish and Seafood

High consumption of fish and seafood, especially fatty fish like sardines, mackerel, and salmon, ensures an intake of omega-3 fatty acids which are known for their cardiovascular benefits.

Moderate Consumption of Poultry and Dairy

While red meat is limited, poultry, eggs, yogurt, and cheese, especially softer varieties like feta, are consumed in moderate amounts.

Wine in Moderation

Wine, especially red, is often consumed with meals. It's taken in moderation, given the potential cardiovascular benefits associated with moderate wine consumption.

Herbs and Spices

Instead of salt, meals are flavored with natural herbs and spices. This not only reduces sodium intake but also introduces several health-promoting compounds into the diet.

Whole Grains

Foods like bread are consumed in their whole form, ensuring a high intake of fiber and other essential nutrients.

Physical Activity

The Mediterranean lifestyle encourages regular physical activity, making it an integral part of daily life.

The Mediterranean diet isn't just a list of foods to consume or avoid; it's a holistic approach to eating and living. Emphasizing wholesome foods, active living, and the importance of community, this diet is as much about quality of life as it is about nutrition.

The health benefits that this cookbook can bring

• Heart Health

The Mediterranean diet, with its rich intake of olive oil, fish, and nuts, is linked to a reduced risk of cardiovascular diseases. It helps lower bad cholesterol and promotes the health of the heart and blood vessels.

• Weight Management

Natural, unprocessed foods, abundant in the diet, combined with portion control and regular physical activity, can aid in sustainable weight loss and prevent obesity.

• Blood Sugar Regulation

The diet is beneficial for blood sugar control, making it a potential ally for those with type 2 diabetes. The high fiber content from whole grains and legumes helps regulate blood sugar spikes.

• Brain Health Preservation

Regular adherence can lead to a reduced risk of cognitive decline and neurodegenerative diseases like Alzheimer's. The omega-3 fatty acids from fish play a crucial role in brain function and health.

• Cancer Risk Reduction

Rich in antioxidants from fruits, vegetables, and olive oil, the Mediterranean diet helps combat oxidative stress, a key player in cancer development.

• Enhanced Gut Health

A diverse range of fruits, vegetables, and whole grains ensures a healthy intake of dietary fiber, promoting a balanced gut microbiome.

• Mood and Mental Health Support

Components of the diet, especially omega-3s and antioxidants, have been linked to a reduced risk of depression and improved mood.

• Bone and Muscle Health

The intake of nutrients like calcium, magnesium, and potassium from the diet supports the health of bones and muscles.

A Mediterranean diet cookbook doesn't just offer recipes; it serves as a guide to a healthier, more fulfilling lifestyle. By embracing its principles, one is investing in a lifetime of health, well-being, and the joy of flavorful, nutritious meals.

28-Day Meal Plan

Day	Breakfast	Lunch	Dinner
1	Zucchini Hummus Wraps 6	Harissa Turkey With Couscous 17	Cheese & Broccoli Quiche 50
2	5-ingredient Quinoa Breakfast Bowls 6	Rosemary Pork Loin With Green Onions 17	Avgolemono (lemon Chicken Soup) 50
3	Fresh Mozzarella & Salmon Frittata 6	Easy Pork Stew 18	Traditional Dukkah Spice 51
4	Apple-tahini Toast 7	Rich Beef Meal 18	Eggplant & Sweet Potato Salad 51
5	Dulse, Avocado, And Tomato Pitas 7	Rosemary Tomato Chicken 18	Chicken And Pastina Soup 52
6	Chickpea Lettuce Wraps 7	Exotic Pork Chops 19	Beef Stew With Green Peas 52
7	Za'atar Pizza 8	Parsley-dijon Chicken And Potatoes 19	Basil Zucchini Marinara 53
8	Baked Parmesan Chicken Wraps 8	Lamb With Couscous & Chickpeas 20	Barley, Parsley, And Pea Salad 53
9	Mediterranean Eggs (shakshuka) 9	Bell Pepper & Onion Pork Chops 20	Favorite Green Bean Stir-fry 53
10	Creamy Vanilla Oatmeal 9	Chicken & Spinach Dish 21	Chicken & Stelline Pasta Soup 54
11	Berry And Nut Parfait 10	Cannellini Bean & Chicken Cassoulet 21	Easy Romesco Sauce 54
12	Banana-blueberry Breakfast Cookies 10	Chicken With Chianti Sauce 22	Yogurt Cucumber Salad 54
13	Apple-oat Porridge With Cranberries 10	Sweet Chicken Stew 22	Roasted Root Vegetable Soup 55
14	Yummy Lentil Stuffed Pitas 11	Picante Beef Stew 22	Fancy Turkish Salad 55

Day	Breakfast	Lunch	Dinner
15	Tomato & Spinach Egg Wraps 11	Baked Anchovies With Chili-garlic Topping 28	Classic Zuppa Toscana 56
16	Avocado And Egg Toast 12	Creamy Trout Spread 28	Mushroom-barley Soup 57
17	Morning Baklava French Toast 12	Chili Flounder Parcels 28	Mushroom & Parmesan Risotto 57
18	Chili & Cheese Frittata 13	Salmon Stuffed Peppers 29	Warm Kale Salad With Red Bell Pepper 58
19	Veg Mix And Blackeye Pea Burritos 13	Bell Pepper & Scallop Skillet 29	Turkish Chickpeas 58
20	Egg & Spinach Pie 14	Tuna Gyros With Tzatziki 30	Homemade Herbes De Provence Spice 58
21	Sweet Banana Pancakes With Strawberries 14	Farro & Trout Bowls With Avocado 30	Bean & Zucchini Soup 59
22	Anchovy & Spinach Sandwiches 14	Shrimp & Spinach A La Puttanesca 31	Sun-dried Tomato & Spinach Pasta Salad 59
23	Creamy Peach Smoothie 15	Crispy Herb Crusted Halibut 31	Restaurant-style Zuppa Di Fagioli 60
24	Avocado Smoothie 15	Andalusian Prawns With Capers 31	Gorgonzola, Fig & Prosciutto Salad 60
25	Vegetable Polenta With Fried Eggs 16	Caper & Squid Stew 32	Artichoke And Arugula Salad 61
26	Creamy Breakfast Bulgur With Berries 16	Fried Scallops With Bean Mash 32	Hot Collard Green Oats With Parmesan 62
27	Tuna Burgers 29	Grilled Sardines With Herby Sauce 33	Veggie & Beef Ragu 62
28	Fried Eggplant Rolls 40	Lemony Trout With Caramelized Shallots 33	Arrabbiata Penne Rigate 63

Measurement Conversions

BASIC KITCHEN CONVERSIONS & EQUIVALENTS

DRY MEASUREMENTS CONVERSION CHART

3 TEASPOONS = 1 TABLESPOON = 1/16 CUP

6 TEASPOONS = 2 TABLESPOONS = 1/8 CUP

12 TEASPOONS = 4 TABLESPOONS = 1/4 CUP

24 TEASPOONS = 8 TABLESPOONS = 1/2 CUP

36 TEASPOONS = 12 TABLESPOONS = 3/4 CUP

48 TEASPOONS = 16 TABLESPOONS = 1 CUP

METRIC TO US COOKING CONVERSIONS

OVEN TEMPERATURES

120 °C = 250 °F

160 °C = 320 °F

180° C = 350 °F

205 °C = 400 °F

220 °C = 425 °F

LIQUID MEASUREMENTS CONVERSION CHART

8 FLUID OUNCES = 1 CUP = 1/2 PINT = 1/4 QUART

16 FLUID OUNCES = 2 CUPS = 1 PINT = 1/2 QUART

32 FLUID OUNCES = 4 CUPS = 2 PINTS = 1 QUART

 = 1/4 GALLON

128 FLUID OUNCES = 16 CUPS = 8 PINTS = 4 QUARTS = 1 GALLON

BAKING IN GRAMS

1 CUP FLOUR = 140 GRAMS

1 CUP SUGAR = 150 GRAMS

1 CUP POWDERED SUGAR = 160 GRAMS

1 CUP HEAVY CREAM = 235 GRAMS

VOLUME

1 MILLILITER = 1/5 TEASPOON

5 ML = 1 TEASPOON

15 ML = 1 TABLESPOON

240 ML = 1 CUP OR 8 FLUID OUNCES

1 LITER = 34 FL. OUNCES

WEIGHT

1 GRAM = .035 OUNCES

100 GRAMS = 3.5 OUNCES

500 GRAMS = 1.1 POUNDS

1 KILOGRAM = 35 OUNCES

US TO METRIC COOKING CONVERSIONS

1/5 TSP = 1 ML

1 TSP = 5 ML

1 TBSP = 15 ML

1 FL OUNCE = 30 ML

1 CUP = 237 ML

1 PINT (2 CUPS) = 473 ML

1 QUART (4 CUPS) = .95 LITER

1 GALLON (16 CUPS) = 3.8 LITERS

1 OZ = 28 GRAMS

1 POUND = 454 GRAMS

BUTTER

1 CUP BUTTER = 2 STICKS = 8 OUNCES = 230 GRAMS = 8 TABLESPOONS

WHAT DOES 1 CUP EQUAL

1 CUP = 8 FLUID OUNCES

1 CUP = 16 TABLESPOONS

1 CUP = 48 TEASPOONS

1 CUP = 1/2 PINT

1 CUP = 1/4 QUART

1 CUP = 1/16 GALLON

1 CUP = 240 ML

BAKING PAN CONVERSIONS

1 CUP ALL-PURPOSE FLOUR = 4.5 OZ

1 CUP ROLLED OATS = 3 OZ 1 LARGE EGG = 1.7 OZ

1 CUP BUTTER = 8 OZ 1 CUP MILK = 8 OZ

1 CUP HEAVY CREAM = 8.4 OZ

1 CUP GRANULATED SUGAR = 7.1 OZ

1 CUP PACKED BROWN SUGAR = 7.75 OZ

1 CUP VEGETABLE OIL = 7.7 OZ

1 CUP UNSIFTED POWDERED SUGAR = 4.4 OZ

BAKING PAN CONVERSIONS

9-INCH ROUND CAKE PAN = 12 CUPS

10-INCH TUBE PAN =16 CUPS

11-INCH BUNDT PAN = 12 CUPS

9-INCH SPRINGFORM PAN = 10 CUPS

9 X 5 INCH LOAF PAN = 8 CUPS

9-INCH SQUARE PAN = 8 CUPS

Breakfast Recipes

Zucchini Hummus Wraps

Servings:2
Cooking Time: 6 Minutes
Ingredients:

- 1 zucchini, ends removed, thinly sliced lengthwise
- ½ teaspoon dried oregano
- ¼ teaspoon freshly ground black pepper
- ¼ teaspoon garlic powder
- ¼ cup hummus
- 2 whole wheat tortillas
- 2 Roma tomatoes, cut lengthwise into slices
- 1 cup chopped kale
- 2 tablespoons chopped red onion
- ½ teaspoon ground cumin

Directions:

1. In a skillet over medium heat, place the zucchini slices and cook for 3 minutes per side. Sprinkle with the oregano, pepper, and garlic powder and remove from the heat.
2. Spread 2 tablespoons of hummus on each tortilla. Lay half the zucchini in the center of each tortilla. Top with tomato slices, kale, red onion, and ¼ teaspoon of cumin. Wrap tightly and serve.

Nutrition Info:

- Info Per Serving: Calories: 248;Fat: 8.1g;Protein: 9.1g;Carbs: 37.1g.

5-ingredient Quinoa Breakfast Bowls

Servings:1
Cooking Time: 17 Minutes
Ingredients:

- ¼ cup quinoa, rinsed
- ¾ cup water, plus additional as needed
- 1 carrot, grated
- ½ small broccoli head, finely chopped
- ¼ teaspoon salt
- 1 tablespoon chopped fresh dill

Directions:

1. Add the quinoa and water to a small pot over high heat and bring to a boil.
2. Once boiling, reduce the heat to low. Cover and cook for 5 minutes, stirring occasionally.
3. Stir in the carrot, broccoli, and salt and continue cooking for 1o to 12 minutes, or until the quinoa is cooked though and the vegetables are fork-tender. If the mixture gets too thick, you can add additional water as needed.
4. Add the dill and serve warm.

Nutrition Info:

- Info Per Serving: Calories: 219;Fat: 2.9g;Protein: 10.0g;Carbs: 40.8g.

Fresh Mozzarella & Salmon Frittata

Servings:4
Cooking Time:15 Minutes
Ingredients:

- 1 ball fresh mozzarella cheese, chopped
- 2 tsp olive oil
- 8 fresh eggs
- ½ cup whole milk
- 1 spring onion, chopped
- ¼ cup chopped fresh basil
- Salt and black pepper to taste
- 3 oz smoked salmon, chopped

Directions:

1. Preheat your broiler to medium. Whisk the eggs with milk, spring onion, basil, pepper, and salt in a bowl. Heat the olive oil in a skillet over medium heat and pour in the egg mixture.
2. Top with mozzarella cheese and cook for 3–5 minutes until the frittata is set on the bottom and the egg is almost set but still moist on top. Scatter over the salmon and place the skillet under the preheated broiler for 1-2 minutes or until set and slightly puffed. Cut the frittata into wedges. Enjoy!

Nutrition Info:

- Info Per Serving: Calories: 351;Fat: 13g;Protein: 52g;Carbs: 6g.

Apple-tahini Toast

Servings:1

Cooking Time: 0 Minutes

Ingredients:

- 2 slices whole-wheat bread, toasted
- 2 tablespoons tahini
- 1 small apple of your choice, cored and thinly sliced
- 1 teaspoon honey

Directions:

1. Spread the tahini on the toasted bread.
2. Place the apple slices on the bread and drizzle with the honey. Serve immediately.

Nutrition Info:

- Info Per Serving: Calories: 458;Fat: 17.8g;Protein: 11.0g;Carbs: 63.5g.

Dulse, Avocado, And Tomato Pitas

Servings:4

Cooking Time: 30 Minutes

Ingredients:

- 2 teaspoons coconut oil
- ½ cup dulse, picked through and separated
- Ground black pepper, to taste
- 2 avocados, sliced
- 2 tablespoons lime juice
- ¼ cup chopped cilantro
- 2 scallions, white and light green parts, sliced
- Sea salt, to taste
- 4 whole wheat pitas, sliced in half
- 4 cups chopped romaine
- 4 plum tomatoes, sliced

Directions:

1. Heat the coconut oil in a nonstick skillet over medium heat until melted.
2. Add the dulse and sauté for 5 minutes or until crispy. Sprinkle with ground black pepper and turn off the heat. Set aside.
3. Put the avocado, lime juice, cilantro, and scallions in a food processor and sprinkle with salt and ground black pepper. Pulse to combine well until smooth.
4. Toast the pitas in a baking pan in the oven for 1 minute until soft.
5. Transfer the pitas to a clean work surface and open. Spread the avocado mixture over the pitas, then top with dulse, romaine, and tomato slices.
6. Serve immediately.

Nutrition Info:

- Info Per Serving: Calories: 412;Fat: 18.7g;Protein: 9.1g;Carbs: 56.1g.

Chickpea Lettuce Wraps

Servings:2

Cooking Time: 0 Minutes

Ingredients:

- 1 can chickpeas, drained and rinsed well
- 1 celery stalk, diced
- ½ shallot, minced
- 1 green apple, cored and diced
- 3 tablespoons tahini (sesame paste)
- 2 teaspoons freshly squeezed lemon juice
- 1 teaspoon raw honey
- 1 teaspoon Dijon mustard
- Dash salt
- Filtered water, to thin
- 4 romaine lettuce leaves

Directions:

1. In a medium bowl, stir together the chickpeas, celery, shallot, apple, tahini, lemon juice, honey, mustard, and salt. If needed, add some water to thin the mixture.
2. Place the romaine lettuce leaves on a plate. Fill each with the chickpea filling, using it all. Wrap the leaves around the filling. Serve immediately.

Nutrition Info:

- Info Per Serving: Calories: 397;Fat: 15.1g;Protein: 15.1g;Carbs: 53.1g.

Za'atar Pizza

Servings:4

Cooking Time: 1o To 12 Minutes

Ingredients:

- 1 sheet puff pastry
- ¼ cup extra-virgin olive oil
- ⅓ cup za'atar seasoning

Directions:

1. Preheat the oven to 350ºF. Line a baking sheet with parchment paper.
2. Place the puff pastry on the prepared baking sheet. Cut the pastry into desired slices.
3. Brush the pastry with the olive oil. Sprinkle with the za'atar seasoning.
4. Put the pastry in the oven and bake for 10 to 12 minutes, or until edges are lightly browned and puffed up.
5. Serve warm.

Nutrition Info:

- Info Per Serving: Calories: 374;Fat: 30.0g;Protein: 3.0g;Carbs: 20.0g.

Baked Parmesan Chicken Wraps

Servings:6

Cooking Time: 18 Minutes

Ingredients:

- 1 pound boneless, skinless chicken breasts
- 1 large egg
- ¼ cup unsweetened almond milk
- ⅔ cup whole-wheat bread crumbs
- ½ cup grated Parmesan cheese
- ¾ teaspoon garlic powder, divided
- 1 cup canned low-sodium or no-salt-added crushed tomatoes
- 1 teaspoon dried oregano
- 6 whole-wheat tortillas, or whole-grain spinach wraps
- 1 cup fresh Mozzarella cheese, sliced
- 1½ cups loosely packed fresh flat-leaf (Italian) parsley, chopped
- Cooking spray

Directions:

1. Preheat the oven to 425ºF. Line a large, rimmed baking sheet with aluminum foil. Place a wire rack on the aluminum foil, and spritz the rack with nonstick cooking spray. Set aside.
2. Place the chicken breasts into a large plastic bag. With a rolling pin, pound the chicken so it is evenly flattened, about ¼ inch thick. Slice the chicken into six portions.
3. In a bowl, whisk together the egg and milk. In another bowl, stir together the bread crumbs, Parmesan cheese and ½ teaspoon of the garlic powder.
4. Dredge each chicken breast portion into the egg mixture, and then into the Parmesan crumb mixture, pressing the crumbs into the chicken so they stick. Arrange the chicken on the prepared wire rack.
5. Bake in the preheated oven for 15 to 18 minutes, or until the internal temperature of the chicken reads 165ºF on a meat thermometer and any juices run clear.
6. Transfer the chicken to a cutting board, and cut each portion diagonally into ½-inch pieces.
7. In a small, microwave-safe bowl, stir together the tomatoes, oregano, and the remaining ¼ teaspoon of the garlic powder. Cover the bowl with a paper towel and microwave for about 1 minute on high, until very hot. Set aside.
8. Wrap the tortillas in a damp paper towel and microwave for 30 to 45 seconds on high, or until warmed through.
9. Assemble the wraps: Divide the chicken slices evenly among the six tortillas and top with the sliced Mozzarella cheese. Spread 1 tablespoon of the warm tomato sauce over the cheese on each tortilla, and top each with about ¼ cup of the parsley.
10. Wrap the tortilla: Fold up the bottom of the tortilla, then fold one side over and fold the other side over the top.
11. Serve the wraps warm with the remaining sauce for dipping.

Nutrition Info:

- Info Per Serving: Calories: 358;Fat: 12.0g;Protein: 21.0g;Carbs: 41.0g.

Mediterranean Eggs (shakshuka)

Servings:4

Cooking Time: 20 Minutes

Ingredients:

- 2 tablespoons extra-virgin olive oil
- 1 cup chopped shallots
- 1 teaspoon garlic powder
- 1 cup finely diced potato
- 1 cup chopped red bell peppers
- 1 can diced tomatoes, drained
- ¼ teaspoon ground cardamom
- ¼ teaspoon paprika
- ¼ teaspoon turmeric
- 4 large eggs
- ¼ cup chopped fresh cilantro

Directions:

1. Preheat the oven to 350°F.
2. Heat the olive oil in an ovenproof skillet over medium-high heat until it shimmers.
3. Add the shallots and sauté for about 3 minutes, stirring occasionally, until fragrant.
4. Fold in the garlic powder, potato, and bell peppers and stir to combine.
5. Cover and cook for 10 minutes, stirring frequently.
6. Add the tomatoes, cardamon, paprika, and turmeric and mix well.
7. When the mixture begins to bubble, remove from the heat and crack the eggs into the skillet.
8. Transfer the skillet to the preheated oven and bake for 5 to 10 minutes, or until the egg whites are set and the yolks are cooked to your liking.
9. Remove from the oven and garnish with the cilantro before serving.

Nutrition Info:

- Info Per Serving: Calories: 223;Fat: 11.8g;Protein: 9.1g;Carbs: 19.5g.

Creamy Vanilla Oatmeal

Servings:4

Cooking Time: 40 Minutes

Ingredients:

- 4 cups water
- Pinch sea salt
- 1 cup steel-cut oats
- ¾ cup unsweetened almond milk
- 2 teaspoons pure vanilla extract

Directions:

1. Add the water and salt to a large saucepan over high heat and bring to a boil.
2. Once boiling, reduce the heat to low and add the oats. Mix well and cook for 30 minutes, stirring occasionally.
3. Fold in the almond milk and vanilla and whisk to combine. Continue cooking for about 10 minutes, or until the oats are thick and creamy.
4. Ladle the oatmeal into bowls and serve warm.

Nutrition Info:

- Info Per Serving: Calories: 117;Fat: 2.2g;Protein: 4.3g;Carbs: 20.0g.

Berry And Nut Parfait

Servings:2

Cooking Time: 0 Minutes

Ingredients:

- 2 cups plain Greek yogurt
- 2 tablespoons honey
- 1 cup fresh raspberries
- 1 cup fresh blueberries
- ½ cup walnut pieces

Directions:

1. In a medium bowl, whisk the yogurt and honey. Spoon into 2 serving bowls.
2. Top each with ½ cup blueberries, ½ cup raspberries, and ¼ cup walnut pieces. Serve immediately.

Nutrition Info:

- Info Per Serving: Calories: 507;Fat: 23.0g;Protein: 24.1g;Carbs: 57.0g.

Banana-blueberry Breakfast Cookies

Servings:4

Cooking Time: 13 Minutes

Ingredients:

- 2 medium bananas, sliced
- 4 tablespoons almond butter
- 4 large eggs, lightly beaten
- ½ cup unsweetened applesauce
- 1 teaspoon vanilla extract
- ⅔ cup coconut flour
- ¼ teaspoon salt
- 1 cup fresh or frozen blueberries

Directions:

1. Preheat the oven to 375ºF. Line a baking sheet with parchment paper.
2. Stir together the bananas and almond butter in a medium bowl until well incorporated.
3. Fold in the beaten eggs, applesauce, and vanilla and blend well.
4. Add the coconut flour and salt and mix well. Add the blueberries and stir to just incorporate.
5. Drop about 2 tablespoons of dough onto the parchment paper-lined baking sheet for each cookie. Using your clean hand, flatten each into a rounded biscuit shape, until it is 1 inch thick.
6. Bake in the preheated oven for about 13 minutes, or until the top is golden brown and a toothpick inserted in the center comes out clean.
7. Let the cookies cool for 5 to 10 minutes before serving.

Nutrition Info:

- Info Per Serving: Calories: 264;Fat: 13.9g;Protein: 7.3g;Carbs: 27.6g.

Apple-oat Porridge With Cranberries

Servings:4

Cooking Time:15 Minutes

Ingredients:

- 3 green apples, cored, peeled and cubed
- 2 cups milk
- ½ cup walnuts, chopped
- 3 tbsp maple syrup
- ½ cup steel cut oats
- ½ tsp cinnamon powder
- ½ cup cranberries, dried
- 1 tsp vanilla extract

Directions:

1. Warm the milk in a pot over medium heat and stir in apples, maple syrup, oats, cinnamon powder, cranberries, vanilla extract, and 1 cup water. Simmer for 10 minutes. Ladle the porridge into serving bowls, top with walnuts, and serve.

Nutrition Info:

- Info Per Serving: Calories: 160;Fat: 3g;Protein: 6g;Carbs: 4g.

Yummy Lentil Stuffed Pitas

Servings:4

Cooking Time:20 Minutes

Ingredients:

- 4 pitta breads, halved horizontally
- 2 tbsp olive oil
- 1 tomato, cubed
- 1 red onion, chopped
- 1 garlic clove, minced
- ¼ cup parsley, chopped
- 1 cup lentils, rinsed
- ¼ cup lemon juice
- Salt and black pepper to taste

Directions:

1. Bring a pot of salted water to a boil over high heat. Pour in the lentils and lower the heat. Cover and let it simmer for 15 minutes or until lentils are tender, adding more water if needed. Drain and set aside.

2. Warm the olive oil in a skillet over medium heat and cook the onion and garlic and for 3 minutes until soft and translucent. Stir in tomato, lemon juice, salt, and pepper and cook for another 10 minutes. Add the lentils and parsley to the skillet and stir to combine. Fill the pita bread with the lentil mixture. Roll up and serve immediately. Enjoy!

Nutrition Info:

- Info Per Serving: Calories: 390;Fat: 2g;Protein: 29g;Carbs: 68g.

Tomato & Spinach Egg Wraps

Servings:2

Cooking Time:15 Minutes

Ingredients:

- 1 tbsp parsley, chopped
- 1 tbsp olive oil
- ¼ onion, chopped
- 3 sun-dried tomatoes, chopped
- 3 large eggs, beaten
- 2 cups baby spinach, torn
- 1 oz feta cheese, crumbled
- Salt to taste
- 2 whole-wheat tortillas, warm

Directions:

1. Warm the olive oil in a pan over medium heat. Sauté the onion and tomatoes for about 3 minutes. Add the beaten eggs and stir to scramble them, about 4 minutes. Add the spinach and parsley stir to combine. Sprinkle the feta cheese over the eggs. Season with salt to taste. Divide the mixture between the tortillas. Roll them up and serve.

Nutrition Info:

- Info Per Serving: Calories: 435;Fat: 28g;Protein: 17g;Carbs: 31g.

Avocado And Egg Toast

Servings:2

Cooking Time: 8 Minutes

Ingredients:

- 2 tablespoons ground flaxseed
- ½ teaspoon baking powder
- 2 large eggs, beaten
- 1 teaspoon salt, plus additional for serving
- ½ teaspoon freshly ground black pepper, plus additional for serving
- ½ teaspoon garlic powder, sesame seed, caraway seed, or other dried herbs (optional)
- 3 tablespoons extra-virgin olive oil, divided
- 1 medium ripe avocado, peeled, pitted, and sliced
- 2 tablespoons chopped ripe tomato

Directions:

1. In a small bowl, combine the flaxseed and baking powder, breaking up any lumps in the baking powder.
2. Add the beaten eggs, salt, pepper, and garlic powder (if desired) and whisk well. Let sit for 2 minutes.
3. In a small nonstick skillet, heat 1 tablespoon of olive oil over medium heat. Pour the egg mixture into the skillet and let cook undisturbed until the egg begins to set on bottom, 2 to 3 minutes.
4. Using a rubber spatula, scrape down the sides to allow uncooked egg to reach the bottom. Cook for an additional 2 to 3 minutes.
5. Once almost set, flip like a pancake and allow the top to fully cook, another 1 to 2 minutes.
6. Remove from the skillet and allow to cool slightly, then slice into 2 pieces.
7. Top each piece with avocado slices, additional salt and pepper, chopped tomato, and drizzle with the remaining 2 tablespoons of olive oil. Serve immediately.

Nutrition Info:

- Info Per Serving: Calories: 297;Fat: 26.1g;Protein: 8.9g;Carbs: 12.0g.

Morning Baklava French Toast

Servings:2

Cooking Time:20 Minutes

Ingredients:

- 2 tbsp orange juice
- 3 fresh eggs, beaten
- 1 tsp lemon zest
- 1/8 tsp vanilla extract
- ¼ cup honey
- 2 tbsp whole milk
- ¾ tsp ground cinnamon
- ¼ cup walnuts, crumbled
- ¼ cup pistachios, crumbled
- 1 tbsp sugar
- 2 tbsp white bread crumbs
- 4 slices bread
- 2 tbsp unsalted butter
- 1 tsp confectioners' sugar

Directions:

1. Combine the eggs, orange juice, lemon zest, vanilla, honey, milk, and cinnamon in a bowl; set aside. Pulse walnuts and pistachios in a food processor until they are finely crumbled. In a small bowl, mix the walnuts, pistachios, sugar, and bread crumbs Spread the nut mixture on 2 bread slices.
2. Cover with the remaining 2 slices. Melt the butter in a skillet over medium heat. Dip the sandwiches into the egg mixture and fry them for 4 minutes on both sides or until golden. Remove to a plate and cut them diagonally. Dust with confectioners' sugar. Serve immediately.

Nutrition Info:

- Info Per Serving: Calories: 651;Fat: 30g;Protein: 21g;Carbs: 80g.

Chili & Cheese Frittata

Servings:6

Cooking Time:35 Minutes

Ingredients:

- 2 tbsp olive oil
- 12 fresh eggs
- ¼ cup half-and-half
- Salt and black pepper to taste
- ½ chili pepper, minced
- 2 ½ cups shredded mozzarella

Directions:

1. Preheat oven to 350 F. Whisk the eggs in a bowl. Add the half-and-half, salt, and black and stir to combine. Warm the olive oil in a skillet over medium heat. Sauté the chili pepper for 2-3 minutes. Sprinkle evenly with mozzarella cheese. Pour eggs over cheese in the skillet. Place the skillet in the oven and bake for 20–25 minutes until just firm. Let cool the frittata for a few minutes and cut into wedges. Serve hot.

Nutrition Info:

- Info Per Serving: Calories: 381;Fat: 31g;Protein: 25g;Carbs: 2g.

Veg Mix And Blackeye Pea Burritos

Servings:6

Cooking Time: 40 Minutes

Ingredients:

- 1 teaspoon olive oil
- 1 red onion, diced
- 2 garlic cloves, minced
- 1 zucchini, chopped
- 1 tomato, diced
- 1 bell pepper, any color, deseeded and diced
- 1 can blackeye peas
- 2 teaspoons chili powder
- Sea salt, to taste
- 6 whole-grain tortillas

Directions:

1. Preheat the oven to 325ºF.
2. Heat the olive oil in a nonstick skillet over medium heat or until shimmering.
3. Add the onion and sauté for 5 minutes or until translucent.
4. Add the garlic and sauté for 30 seconds or until fragrant.
5. Add the zucchini and sauté for 5 minutes or until tender.
6. Add the tomato and bell pepper and sauté for 2 minutes or until soft.
7. Fold in the black peas and sprinkle them with chili powder and salt. Stir to mix well.
8. Place the tortillas on a clean work surface, then top them with sautéed vegetables mix.
9. Fold one ends of tortillas over the vegetable mix, then tuck and roll them into burritos.
10. Arrange the burritos in a baking dish, seam side down, then pour the juice remains in the skillet over the burritos.
11. Bake in the preheated oven for 25 minutes or until golden brown.
12. Serve immediately.

Nutrition Info:

- Info Per Serving: Calories: 335;Fat: 16.2g;Protein: 12.1g;Carbs: 8.3g.

Egg & Spinach Pie

Servings:8
Cooking Time:30 Minutes
Ingredients:

- 2 tbsp olive oil
- 1 onion, chopped
- 1 lb spinach, chopped
- Salt and black pepper to taste
- ¼ tsp ground nutmeg
- 4 large eggs
- 1 cup grated Pecorino cheese
- 2 puff pastry doughs, at room temperature
- 4 hard-boiled eggs, halved

Directions:

1. Preheat the oven to 350 F. Warm the oil in a large skillet over medium heat. Sauté onion for 5 minutes until translucent. Add the spinach and cook for 5 minutes until wilted. Add the garlic salt, pepper, and nutmeg. Set aside to cool.

2. Whish 3 eggs in a small bowl. Pour them over the cooled spinach mixture and sprinkle with ½ cup Pecorino cheese. Roll out one of the pastry doughs on a greased baking sheet.

3. Spread the spinach mix on top, leaving 2 inches around each edge. Top with hard-boiled egg halves, then cover with the second pastry dough. Pinch the edges closed. Beat the remaining egg into a small bowl. Brush the egg wash over the top of the pie. Bake for 15-20 minutes until golden.

Nutrition Info:

- Info Per Serving: Calories: 417;Fat: 28g;Protein: 7g;Carbs: 25g.

Sweet Banana Pancakes With Strawberries

Servings:4
Cooking Time:15 Minutes
Ingredients:

- 2 tbsp olive oil
- 1 cup flour
- 1 cup + 2 tbsp milk
- 2 eggs, beaten
- ⅓ cup honey
- 1 tsp baking soda
- ¼ tsp salt
- 1 sliced banana
- 1 cup sliced strawberries
- 1 tbsp maple syrup

Directions:

1. Mix together the flour, milk, eggs, honey, baking soda, and salt in a bowl. Warm the olive oil in a skillet over medium heat and pour in ⅓ cup of the pancake batter. Cook for 2-3 minutes. Add half of the fresh fruit and flip to cook for 2-3 minutes on the other side until cooked through. Top with the remaining fruit, drizzle with maple syrup and serve.

Nutrition Info:

- Info Per Serving: Calories: 415;Fat: 24g;Protein: 12g;Carbs: 46g.

Anchovy & Spinach Sandwiches

Servings:2
Cooking Time:5 Minutes
Ingredients:

- 1 avocado, mashed
- 4 anchovies, drained
- 4 whole-wheat bread slices
- 1 cup baby spinach
- 1 tomato, sliced

Directions:

1. Spread the slices of bread with avocado mash and arrange the anchovies over. Top with baby spinach and tomato slices.

Nutrition Info:

- Info Per Serving: Calories: 300;Fat: 12g;Protein: 5g;Carbs: 10g.

Creamy Peach Smoothie

Servings:2

Cooking Time: 0 Minutes

Ingredients:

- 2 cups packed frozen peaches, partially thawed
- ½ ripe avocado
- ½ cup plain or vanilla Greek yogurt
- 2 tablespoons flax meal
- 1 tablespoon honey
- 1 teaspoon orange extract
- 1 teaspoon vanilla extract

Directions:

1. Place all the ingredients in a blender and blend until completely mixed and smooth.
2. Divide the mixture into two bowls and serve immediately.

Nutrition Info:

- Info Per Serving: Calories: 212;Fat: 13.1g;Protein: 6.0g;Carbs: 22.5g.

Avocado Smoothie

Servings:2

Cooking Time: 0 Minutes

Ingredients:

- 1 large avocado
- 1½ cups unsweetened coconut milk
- 2 tablespoons honey

Directions:

1. Place all ingredients in a blender and blend until smooth and creamy. Serve immediately.

Nutrition Info:

- Info Per Serving: Calories: 686;Fat: 57.6g;Protein: 6.2g;Carbs: 35.8g.

Vegetable Polenta With Fried Eggs

Servings:4
Cooking Time:35 Minutes
Ingredients:

- 2 tbsp butter
- ½ tsp sea salt
- 1 cup polenta
- 4 eggs
- 2 spring onions, chopped
- 1 bell pepper, chopped
- 1 zucchini, chopped
- 1 tsp ginger-garlic paste
- 1 ½ cups vegetable broth
- ¼ tsp chili flakes, crushed
- 2 tbsp basil leaves, chopped

Directions:

1. Melt 1 tbsp of the butter in a skillet over medium heat. Place in spring onions, ginger-garlic paste, bell pepper, and zucchini and sauté for 5 minutes; set aside.
2. Pour the broth and 1 ½ cups of water in a pot and bring to a boil. Gradually whisk in polenta to avoid chunks, lower the heat, and simmer for 4-5 minutes. Keep whisking until it begins to thicken. Cook covered for 20 minutes, stirring often. Add the zucchini mixture, chili flakes, and salt and stir.
3. Heat the remaining butter in a skillet. Break the eggs and fry them until set and well cooked. Divide the polenta between bowls top with fried eggs and basil, and serve.

Nutrition Info:

- Info Per Serving: Calories: 295;Fat: 12g;Protein: 11g;Carbs: 36g.

Creamy Breakfast Bulgur With Berries

Servings:2
Cooking Time: 10 Minutes
Ingredients:

- ½ cup medium-grain bulgur wheat
- 1 cup water
- Pinch sea salt
- ¼ cup unsweetened almond milk
- 1 teaspoon pure vanilla extract
- ¼ teaspoon ground cinnamon
- 1 cup fresh berries of your choice

Directions:

1. Put the bulgur in a medium saucepan with the water and sea salt, and bring to a boil.
2. Cover, remove from heat, and let stand for 10 minutes until water is absorbed.
3. Stir in the milk, vanilla, and cinnamon until fully incorporated. Divide between 2 bowls and top with the fresh berries to serve.

Nutrition Info:

- Info Per Serving: Calories: 173;Fat: 1.6g;Protein: 5.7g;Carbs: 34.0g.

Poultry And Meats Recipes

<u>Harissa Turkey With Couscous</u>

Servings:4
Cooking Time:20 Min + Marinating Time
Ingredients:
- 1 lb skinless turkey breast slices
- 2 tbsp olive oil
- 1 tsp garlic powder
- ½ tsp ground coriander
- 1 tbsp harissa seasoning
- 1 cup couscous
- 2 tbsp raisins, soaked
- 2 tbsp chopped parsley
- Salt and black pepper to taste

Directions:

1. Whisk the olive oil, garlic powder, ground coriander, harissa, salt, and pepper in a bowl. Add the turkey slices and toss to coat. Marinate covered for 30 minutes. Place the couscous in a large bowl and pour 1 ½ cups of salted boiling water. Cover and leave to sit for 5 minutes. Fluff with a fork and stir in raisins and parsley. Keep warm until ready to serve.

2. Preheat your grill to high. Place the turkey slices on the grill and cook for 3 minutes per side until cooked through with no pink showing. Serve with the couscous.

Nutrition Info:
- Info Per Serving: Calories: 350;Fat: 7g;Protein: 47g;Carbs: 19g.

<u>Rosemary Pork Loin With Green Onions</u>

Servings:4
Cooking Time:50 Minutes
Ingredients:
- 2 lb pork loin roast, boneless and cubed
- 2 tbsp olive oil
- 2 garlic cloves, minced
- Salt and black pepper to taste
- 1 cup tomato sauce
- 1 tsp rosemary, chopped
- 4 green onions, chopped

Directions:

1. Preheat the oven to 360 F. Heat olive oil in a skillet over medium heat and cook pork, garlic, and green onions for 6-7 minutes, stirring often. Add in tomato sauce, rosemary, and 1 cup of water. Season with salt and pepper. Transfer to a baking dish and bake for 40 minutes. Serve warm.

Nutrition Info:
- Info Per Serving: Calories: 280;Fat: 16g;Protein: 19g;Carbs: 18g.

Easy Pork Stew

Servings:4
Cooking Time:35 Minutes
Ingredients:

- 2 tbsp olive oil
- 1 lb pork shoulder, cubed
- Salt and black pepper to taste
- 1 onion, chopped
- 2 garlic cloves, minced
- 1 tbsp chili paste
- 2 tbsp balsamic vinegar
- ¼ cup chicken stock
- ¼ cup mint, chopped

Directions:

1. Warm the olive oil in a skillet over medium heat and cook onion for 3 minutes. Put in pork cubes and cook for another 3 minutes. Stir in salt, pepper, garlic, chili paste, vinegar, stock, and mint and cook for an additional 20-25 minutes.

Nutrition Info:

- Info Per Serving: Calories: 310;Fat: 14g;Protein: 20g;Carbs: 16g.

Rich Beef Meal

Servings:4
Cooking Time:40 Minutes
Ingredients:

- 1 tbsp olive oil
- 1 lb beef meat, cubed
- 1 red onion, chopped
- 1 garlic clove, minced
- 1 celery stalk, chopped
- Salt and black pepper to taste
- 14 oz canned tomatoes, diced
- 1 cup vegetable stock
- ½ tsp ground nutmeg
- 2 tsp dill, chopped

Directions:

1. Warm the olive oil in a skillet over medium heat and cook onion and garlic for 5 minutes. Put in beef and cook for 5 more minutes. Stir in celery, salt, pepper, tomatoes, stock, nutmeg, and dill and bring to a boil. Cook for 20 minutes.

Nutrition Info:

- Info Per Serving: Calories: 300;Fat: 14g;Protein: 19g;Carbs: 16g.

Rosemary Tomato Chicken

Servings:4
Cooking Time:50 Minutes
Ingredients:

- 2 tbsp olive oil
- 1 lb chicken breasts, sliced
- 1 onion, chopped
- 1 carrot, chopped
- 2 garlic cloves, minced
- ½ cup chicken stock
- 1 tsp oregano, dried
- 1 tsp tarragon, dried
- 1 tsp rosemary, dried
- 1 cup canned tomatoes, diced
- Salt and black pepper to taste

Directions:

1. Warm the olive oil in a pot over medium heat and cook the chicken for 8 minutes on both sides. Put in carrot, garlic, and onion and cook for an additional 3 minutes. Season with salt and pepper. Pour in stock, oregano, tarragon, rosemary, and tomatoes and bring to a boil; simmer for 25 minutes. Serve.

Nutrition Info:

- Info Per Serving: Calories: 260;Fat: 12g;Protein: 10g;Carbs: 16g.

Exotic Pork Chops

Servings:4

Cooking Time:35 Minutes

Ingredients:

- 2 tbsp olive oil
- 2 cups chicken stock
- 2 garlic cloves, minced
- 4 pork loin chops, boneless
- 2 spring onions, chopped
- 2 mangos, peeled and cubed
- 1 tsp sweet paprika
- Salt and black pepper to taste
- ½ tsp dried oregano

Directions:

1. Warm the olive oil in a skillet over medium heat and sear pork chops for 4 minutes on both sides. Put in onions and garlic and cook for another 3 minutes. Stir in mangos, paprika, salt, pepper, oregano, and chicken stock and cook for 15 minutes, stirring often. Serve immediately.

Nutrition Info:

- Info Per Serving: Calories: 310;Fat: 15g;Protein: 25g;Carbs: 13g.

Parsley-dijon Chicken And Potatoes

Servings:6

Cooking Time: 22 Minutes

Ingredients:

- 1 tablespoon extra-virgin olive oil
- 1½ pounds boneless, skinless chicken thighs, cut into 1-inch cubes, patted dry
- 1½ pounds Yukon Gold potatoes, unpeeled, cut into ½-inch cubes
- 2 garlic cloves, minced
- ¼ cup dry white wine
- 1 cup low-sodium or no-salt-added chicken broth
- 1 tablespoon Dijon mustard
- ¼ teaspoon freshly ground black pepper
- ¼ teaspoon kosher or sea salt
- 1 cup chopped fresh flat-leaf (Italian) parsley, including stems
- 1 tablespoon freshly squeezed lemon juice

Directions:

1. In a large skillet over medium-high heat, heat the oil. Add the chicken and cook for 5 minutes, stirring only after the chicken has browned on one side. Remove the chicken and reserve on a plate.

2. Add the potatoes to the skillet and cook for 5 minutes, stirring only after the potatoes have become golden and crispy on one side. Push the potatoes to the side of the skillet, add the garlic, and cook, stirring constantly, for 1 minute. Add the wine and cook for 1 minute, until nearly evaporated. Add the chicken broth, mustard, salt, pepper, and reserved chicken. Turn the heat to high and bring to a boil.

3. Once boiling, cover, reduce the heat to medium-low, and cook for 10 to 12 minutes, until the potatoes are tender and the internal temperature of the chicken measures 165ºF on a meat thermometer and any juices run clear.

4. During the last minute of cooking, stir in the parsley. Remove from the heat, stir in the lemon juice, and serve.

Nutrition Info:

- Info Per Serving: Calories: 324;Fat: 9.0g;Protein: 16.0g;Carbs: 45.0g.

Lamb With Couscous & Chickpeas

Servings:6
Cooking Time:50 Minutes

Ingredients:

- 1 lb lamb shoulder, halved
- 3 tbsp olive oil
- 1 cup couscous
- Salt and black pepper to taste
- 1 onion, finely chopped
- 10 strips orange zest
- 1 tsp ground coriander
- ¼ tsp ground cinnamon
- ½ tsp cayenne pepper
- ½ cup dry white wine
- 2 ½ cups chicken broth
- 1 can chickpeas
- ½ cup dates, chopped
- ½ cup sliced almonds, toasted

Directions:

1. Cover the couscous in a bowl with 1 ½ cups of boiling water and put a lid. Let stand for 5 minutes to absorb the water.

2. Preheat oven to 330 F. Heat 2 tablespoons oil in a pot over medium heat. Season the lamb with salt and pepper and brown it for 4 minutes per side; set aside.

3. Stir-fry onion into the fat left in the pot, 3 minutes. Stir in orange zest, coriander, cinnamon, cayenne, and pepper until fragrant 30 seconds. Stir in wine, scraping off any browned bits. Stir in broth and chickpeas and bring to a boil.

4. Make a nestle of lamb into the pot along with any accumulated juices. Cover, transfer the pot in the oven, and cook until fork slips easily in and out of the lamb, 1 hour.

5. Transfer the lamb to cutting board, let cool slightly, then shred using 2 forks, discarding excess fat and bones. Strain cooking liquid through a fine mesh strainer set over the bowl. Return solids and 1 ½ cups of cooking liquid to the pot and bring to a simmer over medium heat; discard the remaining liquid. Stir in couscous and dates. Add shredded lamb and almonds. Season to taste and serve.

Nutrition Info:

- Info Per Serving: Calories: 555;Fat: 31g;Protein: 37g;Carbs: 42g.

Bell Pepper & Onion Pork Chops

Servings:4
Cooking Time:30 Minutes

Ingredients:

- 2 tbsp olive oil
- 4 pork chops
- Salt and black pepper to taste
- 1 tsp fennel seeds
- 1 red bell pepper, sliced
- 1 green bell pepper, sliced
- 1 yellow onion, thinly sliced
- 2 tsp Italian seasoning
- 2 garlic cloves, minced
- 1 tbsp balsamic vinegar

Directions:

1. Warm the olive oil in a large skillet over medium heat. Season the pork chops with salt and pepper and add them to the skillet. Cook for 6-8 minutes on both sides or until golden brown; reserve. Sauté the garlic, sliced bell peppers, onions, fennel seeds, and herbs in the skillet for 6-8 minutes until tender, stirring occasionally. Return the pork, cover, and lower the heat to low. Cook for another 3 minutes or until the pork is cooked through. Transfer the pork and vegetables to a serving platter. Add the vinegar to the skillet and stir to combine for 1-2 minutes. Drizzle the sauce over the pork.

Nutrition Info:

- Info Per Serving: Calories: 508;Fat: 40g;Protein: 31g;Carbs: 8g.

Chicken & Spinach Dish

Servings:4

Cooking Time:60 Minutes

Ingredients:

- 2 tbsp olive oil
- 2 cups baby spinach
- 1 lb chicken sausage, sliced
- 1 red bell pepper, chopped
- 1 onion, sliced
- 2 tbsp garlic, minced
- Salt and black pepper to taste
- ½ cup chicken stock
- 1 tbsp balsamic vinegar

Directions:

1. Preheat oven to 380 F. Warm olive oil in a skillet over medium heat. Cook sausages for 6 minutes on all sides. Remove to a bowl. Add the bell pepper, onion, garlic, salt, pepper to the skillet and sauté for 5 minutes. Pour in stock and vinegar and return the sausages. Bring to a boil and cook for 10 minutes. Add in the spinach and cook until wilts, about 4 minutes. Serve and enjoy!

Nutrition Info:

- Info Per Serving: Calories: 300;Fat: 15g;Protein: 27g;Carbs: 18g.

Cannellini Bean & Chicken Cassoulet

Servings:4

Cooking Time:40 Minutes

Ingredients:

- 1 lb chicken thighs, boneless and skinless
- 2 tbsp olive oil
- 2 tbsp tomato paste
- 1 celery stalk, chopped
- 1 sweet onion, chopped
- 2 garlic cloves, chopped
- ½ cup chicken stock
- 14 oz canned cannellini beans
- Salt and black pepper to taste

Directions:

1. Warm the olive oil in a pot over medium heat. Cook onion, celery, and garlic for 3 minutes. Put in chicken and cook for 6 minutes on all sides. Stir in tomato paste, stock, beans, salt, and pepper and bring to a boil. Cook for 30 minutes.

Nutrition Info:

- Info Per Serving: Calories: 260;Fat: 11g;Protein: 25g;Carbs: 26g.

Chicken With Chianti Sauce

Servings:4

Cooking Time:80 Min + Chilling Time

Ingredients:

- 4 tbsp olive oil
- 2 tbsp butter
- 3 garlic cloves, minced
- 1 tbsp lemon zest
- 2 tbsp fresh thyme, chopped
- 2 tbsp fresh parsley, chopped
- Salt and black pepper to taste
- 4 bone-in chicken legs
- 2 cups red grapes (in clusters)
- 1 red onion, sliced
- 1 cup Chianti red wine
- 1 cup chicken stock

Directions:

1. Toss the chicken with 2 tbsp of olive oil, garlic, thyme, parsley, lemon zest, salt, and pepper in a bowl. Refrigerate for 1 hour. Preheat oven to 400 F. Heat the remaining olive oil in a saucepan over medium heat. Sear the chicken for 3–4 minutes per side. Top chicken with the grapes. Transfer to the oven and bake for 20–30 minutes or until internal temperature registers 180 F on an instant-read thermometer.

2. Melt the butter in another saucepan and sauté the onion for 3–4 minutes. Add the wine and stock, stir, and simmer the sauce for about 30 minutes until it is thickened. Plate the chicken and grapes and pour the sauce over to serve.

Nutrition Info:

- Info Per Serving: Calories: 562;Fat: 31g;Protein: 52g;Carbs: 16g.

Sweet Chicken Stew

Servings:4

Cooking Time:50 Minutes

Ingredients:

- 2 tbsp olive oil
- 3 garlic cloves, minced
- 3 tbsp cilantro, chopped
- Salt and black pepper to taste
- 2 cups chicken stock
- 2 shallots, thinly sliced
- 1 lb chicken breasts, cubed
- 5 oz dried pitted prunes, halved

Directions:

1. Warm the olive oil in a pot over medium heat and cook shallots and garlic for 3 minutes. Add in chicken breasts and cook for another 5 minutes, stirring occasionally. Pour in chicken stock and prunes and season with salt and pepper. Cook for 30 minutes. Garnish with cilantro and serve.

Nutrition Info:

- Info Per Serving: Calories: 310;Fat: 26g;Protein: 7g;Carbs: 16g.

Picante Beef Stew

Servings:4

Cooking Time:35 Minutes

Ingredients:

- 2 tbsp olive oil
- 1 carrot, chopped
- 4 potatoes, diced
- 1 tsp ground nutmeg
- ½ tsp cinnamon
- 1 lb beef stew meat, cubed
- ½ cup sweet chili sauce
- ½ cup vegetable stock
- 1 tbsp cilantro, chopped
- Salt and black pepper to taste

Directions:

1. Warm the olive oil in a skillet over medium heat and sear beef for 5 minutes. Stir in chili sauce, carrot, potatoes, stock, nutmeg, cinnamon, cilantro, salt, and pepper and bring to a boil. Cook for another 20 minutes. Serve immediately.

Nutrition Info:

- Info Per Serving: Calories: 300;Fat: 22g;Protein: 20g;Carbs: 26g.

Beef & Bell Pepper Bake

Servings:4

Cooking Time:1 Hour 40 Minutes

Ingredients:

- 2 tbsp olive oil
- 1 lb beef steaks
- 1 red bell pepper, sliced
- 1 green bell pepper, sliced
- 1 yellow bell pepper, sliced
- 2 tbsp oregano, chopped
- 4 garlic cloves, minced
- ½ cup chicken stock
- Salt and black pepper to taste

Directions:

1. Preheat oven to 360 F. Warm olive oil in a skillet over medium heat. Sear the beef steaks for 8 minutes on both sides. Stir in bell peppers, oregano, garlic, stock, salt, and pepper and bake for 80 minutes. Serve warm.

Nutrition Info:

- Info Per Serving: Calories: 310;Fat: 15g;Protein: 25g;Carbs: 17g.

Syrupy Chicken Breasts

Servings:4

Cooking Time:30 Minutes

Ingredients:

- 2 tbsp olive oil
- 2 cups peaches, cubed
- 1 tbsp smoked paprika
- 1 lb chicken breasts, cubed
- 2 cups chicken broth
- Salt and black pepper to taste
- 1 tbsp chives, chopped

Directions:

1. Warm the olive oil in a skillet over medium heat and sauté chicken, salt, and pepper for 8 minutes, stirring occasionally. Stir in peaches, paprika, and chicken broth and cook for another 15 minutes. Serve topped with chives.

Nutrition Info:

- Info Per Serving: Calories: 280;Fat: 14g;Protein: 17g;Carbs: 26g.

Quinoa & Chicken Bowl

Servings:4

Cooking Time:50 Minutes

Ingredients:

- 4 chicken things, skinless and boneless
- 2 tbsp olive oil
- Salt and black pepper to taste
- 1 celery stalk, chopped
- 2 leeks, chopped
- 2 cups chicken stock
- 2 tbsp cilantro, chopped
- 1 cup quinoa
- 1 tsp lemon zest

Directions:

1. Warm the olive oil in a pot over medium heat and cook the chicken for 6-8 minutes on all sides. Stir in leeks and celery and cook for another 5 minutes until tender. Season with salt and pepper. Stir in quinoa and lemon zest for 1 minute and pour in the chicken stock. Bring to a boil and simmer for 35 minutes. Serve topped with cilantro.

Nutrition Info:

- Info Per Serving: Calories: 250;Fat: 14g;Protein: 35g;Carbs: 17g.

Cilantro Turkey Penne With Asparagus

Servings:4
Cooking Time:40 Minutes

Ingredients:

- 3 tbsp olive oil
- 16 oz penne pasta
- 1 lb turkey breast strips
- 1 lb asparagus, chopped
- 1 tsp basil, chopped
- Salt and black pepper to taste
- ½ cup tomato sauce
- 2 tbsp cilantro, chopped

Directions:

1. Bring to a boil salted water in a pot over medium heat and cook penne until "al dente", 8-10 minutes. Drain and set aside; reserve 1 cup of the cooking water.

2. Warm the olive oil in a skillet over medium heat and sear turkey for 4 minutes, stirring periodically. Add in asparagus and sauté for 3-4 more minutes. Pour in the tomato sauce and reserved pasta liquid and bring to a boil; simmer for 20 minutes. Stir in cooked penne, season with salt and pepper, and top with the basil and cilantro to serve.

Nutrition Info:

- Info Per Serving: Calories: 350;Fat: 22g;Protein: 19g;Carbs: 23g.

Saucy Turkey With Ricotta Cheese

Servings:4
Cooking Time:60 Minutes

Ingredients:

- 2 tbsp olive oil
- 1 turkey breast, cubed
- 1 ½ cups salsa verde
- Salt and black pepper to taste
- 4 oz ricotta cheese, crumbled
- 2 tbsp cilantro, chopped

Directions:

1. Preheat the oven to 380 F. Grease a roasting pan with oil. In a bowl, place turkey, salsa verde, salt, and pepper and toss to coat. Transfer to the roasting pan and bake for 50 minutes. Top with ricotta cheese and cilantro and serve.

Nutrition Info:

- Info Per Serving: Calories: 340;Fat: 16g;Protein: 35g;Carbs: 23g.

Cocktail Meatballs In Almond Sauce

Servings:4
Cooking Time:30 Minutes

Ingredients:

- 3 tbsp olive oil
- 8 oz ground pork
- 8 oz ground beef
- ½ cup finely minced onions
- 1 large egg, beaten
- 1 potato, shredded
- Salt and black pepper to taste
- 1 tsp garlic powder
- ½ tsp oregano
- 2 tbsp chopped parsley
- ¼ cup ground almonds
- 1 cup chicken broth
- ¼ cup butter

Directions:

1. Place the ground meat, onions, egg, potato, salt, garlic powder, pepper, and oregano in a large bowl. Shape the mixture into small meatballs, about 1 inch in diameter, and place on a plate. Let sit for 10 minutes at room temperature.

2. Warm the olive oil in a skillet over medium heat. Add the meatballs and brown them for 6-8 minutes on all sides; reserve. In the hot skillet, melt the butter and add the almonds and broth. Cook for 3-5 minutes. Add the meatballs to the skillet, cover, and cook for 8-10 minutes. Top with parsley.

Nutrition Info:

- Info Per Serving: Calories: 449;Fat: 42g;Protein: 16g;Carbs: 3g.

Greek-style Chicken With Potatoes

Servings:4

Cooking Time:30 Minutes

Ingredients:

- 4 potatoes, peeled and quartered
- 4 boneless skinless chicken drumsticks
- 4 cups water
- 2 lemons, zested and juiced
- 1 tbsp olive oil
- 2 tsp fresh oregano
- Salt and black pepper to taste
- 2 Serrano peppers, minced
- 3 tbsp finely chopped parsley
- 1 cup packed watercress
- 1 cucumber, thinly chopped
- 10 cherry tomatoes, quartered
- 16 Kalamata olives, pitted
- ¼ cup hummus
- ¼ cup feta cheese, crumbled
- Lemon wedges, for serving

Directions:

1.   Add water and potatoes to your Instant Pot. Set trivet over them. In a baking bowl, mix lemon juice, olive oil, black pepper, oregano, zest, salt, and Serrano peppers. Add chicken drumsticks in the marinade and stir to coat.

2.   Set the bowl with chicken on the trivet in the cooker. Seal the lid, select Manual and cook on High for 15 minutes. Do a quick release. Take out the bowl with chicken and the trivet from the pot. Drain potatoes and add parsley and salt. Split the potatoes among serving plates and top with watercress, cucumber slices, hummus, cherry tomatoes, chicken, olives, and feta cheese. Garnish with lemon wedges. Serve.

Nutrition Info:

- Info Per Serving: Calories: 726;Fat: 15g;Protein: 72g;Carbs: 75g.

Sweet Pork Stew

Servings:4

Cooking Time:50 Minutes

Ingredients:

- 3 tbsp olive oil
- 1 ½ lb pork stew meat, cubed
- Salt and black pepper to taste
- 1 cup red onions, chopped
- 1 cup dried apricots, chopped
- 2 garlic cloves, minced
- 1 cup canned tomatoes, diced
- 2 tbsp parsley, chopped

Directions:

1.   Warm olive oil in a skillet over medium heat. Sear pork meat for 5 minutes. Put in onions and cook for another 5 minutes. Stir in salt, pepper, apricots, garlic, tomatoes, and parsley and bring to a simmer and cook for an additional 30 minutes.

Nutrition Info:

- Info Per Serving: Calories: 320;Fat: 17g;Protein: 35g;Carbs: 22g.

Pork Chops With Squash & Zucchini

Servings:4

Cooking Time:40 Minutes

Ingredients:

- 2 tbsp olive oil
- 4 pork loin chops, boneless
- 1 tsp Italian seasoning
- 1 zucchini, sliced
- 1 yellow squash, cubed
- 10 cherry tomatoes, halved
- ½ tsp oregano, dried
- Salt and black pepper to taste
- 3 garlic cloves, minced
- 10 Kalamata olives, halved
- ¼ cup ricotta cheese, crumbled

Directions:

1. Preheat the oven to 370 F. Place pork chops, salt, pepper, Italian seasoning, zucchini, squash, tomatoes, oregano, olive oil, garlic, and olives in a roasting pan and bake covered for 30 minutes. Serve topped with ricotta cheese.

Nutrition Info:

- Info Per Serving: Calories: 240;Fat: 10g;Protein: 29g;Carbs: 10g.

Spiced Beef Meatballs

Servings:4

Cooking Time:25 Minutes

Ingredients:

- ¼ cup fresh mozzarella cheese, crumbled
- 1 lb ground beef
- ¼ cup panko breadcrumbs
- Salt and black pepper to taste
- 1 red onion, grated
- 2 tbsp parsley, chopped
- 2 garlic cloves, minced
- 1 lemon, juiced and zested
- 1 egg
- ½ tsp ground cumin
- ½ tsp ground coriander
- ¼ tsp cinnamon powder

Directions:

1. Preheat oven to 390 F. Line a baking sheet with parchment paper. Combine beef, breadcrumbs, salt, pepper, onion, parsley, garlic, lemon juice, lemon zest, egg, cumin, coriander, cinnamon powder, and fresh mozzarella cheese in a bowl and form balls out of the mixture. Place meatballs on the sheet and bake for 15 minutes. Serve warm.

Nutrition Info:

- Info Per Serving: Calories: 310;Fat: 16g;Protein: 36g;Carbs: 23g.

Garlicky Beef With Walnuts

Servings:4

Cooking Time:30 Minutes

Ingredients:

- 3 tbsp olive oil
- 1 ½ lb beef meat, cubed
- 2 tbsp lime juice
- 1 tbsp balsamic vinegar
- 5 garlic cloves, minced
- Salt and black pepper to taste
- 2 tbsp walnuts, chopped
- 2 scallions, chopped

Directions:

1. Warm the olive oil in a skillet over medium heat and sear beef for 8 minutes on both sides. Put in scallions and garlic and cook for another 2 minutes. Stir in lime juice, vinegar, salt, pepper, and walnuts and cook for an additional 10 minutes.

Nutrition Info:

- Info Per Serving: Calories: 310;Fat: 15g;Protein: 19g;Carbs: 17g.

Apricot-glazed Pork Skewers

Servings:6

Cooking Time:50 Minutes

Ingredients:

- 2 lb pork tenderloin, cubed
- 1 cup apricot jam
- ½ cup apricot nectar
- 1 cup dried whole apricots
- 2 onions, cut into wedges
- ½ tsp dried rosemary

Directions:

1. Coat the pork cubes with apricot jam, cover, and set aside for 10-15 minutes. Bring to a boil the apricot nectar, rosemary, and dried apricots in a saucepan over medium heat. Lower the heat and simmer for 2-3 minutes. Remove the apricots with a perforated spoon and pour the hot liquid over the pork. Stir and drain the pork, reserving the marinade.

2. Preheat your grill to medium-high. Alternate pork cubes, onion wedges, and apricots onto 6 metal skewers. Brush them with some marinade and grill for 10-12 minutes, turning and brushing with some more marinade until the pork is slightly pink and onions are crisp-tender. Simmer the remaining marinade for 3-5 minutes. Serve the skewers with marinade on the side.

Nutrition Info:

- Info Per Serving: Calories: 393;Fat: 4g;Protein: 34g;Carbs: 59g.

Fish And Seafood Recipes

Baked Anchovies With Chili-garlic Topping

Servings:2
Cooking Time:10 Minutes
Ingredients:
- ½ tsp red pepper flakes
- 16 canned anchovies
- 4 garlic cloves, minced
- Salt and black pepper to taste

Directions:
1. Preheat the broiler. Arrange the anchovies on a foil-lined baking dish. In a bowl, mix anchovy olive oil, garlic, salt, red flakes, and pepper and pour over anchovies. Broil for 3-4 minutes. Divide between 4 plates and drizzle with the remaining mixture from the dish. Serve and enjoy!

Nutrition Info:
- Info Per Serving: Calories: 103;Fat: 3g;Protein: 11g;Carbs: 5g.

Creamy Trout Spread

Servings:4
Cooking Time:5 Minutes
Ingredients:
- 2 tbsp olive oil
- 1 cup Greek yogurt
- 2 oz smoked trout, flaked
- 1 tbsp lemon juice
- 2 tbsp chives, chopped
- Salt and black pepper to taste

Directions:
1. Place trout, lemon juice, yogurt, chives, salt, pepper, and olive oil in a bowl and toss to combine. Serve with crackers.

Nutrition Info:
- Info Per Serving: Calories: 270;Fat: 5g;Protein: 8g;Carbs: 6g.

Chili Flounder Parcels

Servings:4
Cooking Time:20 Minutes
Ingredients:
- 2 tbsp olive oil
- 4 flounder fillets
- ¼ tsp red pepper flakes
- 4 fresh rosemary sprigs
- 2 garlic cloves, thinly sliced
- 1 cup cherry tomatoes, halved
- ½ chopped onion
- 2 tbsp capers
- 8 black olives, sliced
- 2 tbsp dry white wine
- Salt and black pepper to taste

Directions:
1. Preheat oven to 420 F. Drizzle the flounder with olive oil and season with salt, pepper, and red pepper flakes. Divide fillets between 4 pieces of aluminium foil. Top each one with garlic, cherry tomatoes, capers, onion, and olives. Fold the edges to form packets with opened tops. Add in a rosemary sprig in each one and drizzle with the white wine. Seal the packets and arrange them on a baking sheet. Bake for 10 minutes or until the fish is cooked. Serve warm.

Nutrition Info:
- Info Per Serving: Calories: 242;Fat: 10g;Protein: 31.5g;Carbs: 4g.

Salmon Stuffed Peppers

Servings:4

Cooking Time:25 Minutes

Ingredients:

- 4 bell peppers
- 10 oz canned salmon, drained
- 12 black olives, chopped
- 1 red onion, finely chopped
- ½ tsp garlic, minced
- 1/3 cup mayonnaise
- 1 cup cream cheese
- 1 tsp Mediterranean seasoning
- Salt and pepper flakes to taste

Directions:

1. Preheat oven to 390 F. Cut the peppers into halves and remove the seeds. In a mixing bowl, combine the salmon, onion, garlic, mayonnaise, olives, salt, red pepper, Mediterranean spice mix, and cream cheese. Divide the mixture between the peppers and bake them in the oven for 10-12 minutes or until cooked through. Serve and enjoy!

Nutrition Info:

- Info Per Serving: Calories: 272;Fat: 14g;Protein: 29g;Carbs: 5g.

Bell Pepper & Scallop Skillet

Servings:4

Cooking Time:25 Minutes

Ingredients:

- 3 tbsp olive oil
- 2 celery stalks, sliced
- 2 lb sea scallops, halved
- 3 garlic cloves, minced
- Juice of 1 lime
- 1 red bell pepper, chopped
- 1 tbsp capers, chopped
- 1 tbsp mayonnaise
- 1 tbsp rosemary, chopped
- 1 cup chicken stock

Directions:

1. Warm olive oil in a skillet over medium heat and cook celery and garlic for 2 minutes. Stir in bell pepper, lime juice, capers, rosemary, and stock and bring to a boil. Simmer for 8 minutes. Mix in scallops and mayonnaise and cook for 5 minutes.

Nutrition Info:

- Info Per Serving: Calories: 310;Fat: 16g;Protein: 9g;Carbs: 33g.

Tuna Burgers

Servings:4

Cooking Time:20 Minutes

Ingredients:

- 2 tbsp olive oil
- 2 cans tuna, flaked
- 4 hamburger buns
- 3 green onions, chopped
- ¼ cup breadcrumbs
- 1 egg, beaten
- 2 tbsp chopped fresh parsley
- 1 tbsp Italian seasoning
- 1 lemon, zested
- ½ cup mayonnaise
- 1 tbsp chopped fresh dill
- 1 tbsp green olives, chopped
- Sea salt to taste

Directions:

1. Combine tuna, breadcrumbs, green onions, eggs, Italian seasoning, parsley, and lemon zest in a bowl. Shape the mixture into 6 patties. Warm olive oil in a skillet over medium heat and brown patties for 8 minutes on both sides. Mix mayonnaise, green olives, dill, and salt in a bowl. Spoon the mixture on the buns and top with the patties.

Nutrition Info:

- Info Per Serving: Calories: 423;Fat: 24g;Protein: 16g;Carbs: 35g.

Tuna Gyros With Tzatziki

Servings:4
Cooking Time:15 Minutes
Ingredients:

- 4 oz tzatziki
- ½ lb canned tuna, drained
- ½ cup tahini
- 4 sundried tomatoes, diced
- 2 tbsp warm water
- 2 garlic cloves, minced
- 1 tbsp lemon juice
- 4 pita wraps
- 5 black olives, chopped
- Salt and black pepper to taste

Directions:

1. In a bowl, combine the tahini, water, garlic, lemon juice, salt, and black pepper. Warm the pita wraps in a grilled pan for a few minutes, turning once. Spread the tahini and tzatziki sauces over the warmed pitas and top with tuna, sundried tomatoes, and olives. Fold in half and serve immediately.

Nutrition Info:

- Info Per Serving: Calories: 334;Fat: 24g;Protein: 21.3g;Carbs: 9g.

Farro & Trout Bowls With Avocado

Servings:4
Cooking Time:50 Minutes
Ingredients:

- 4 tbsp olive oil
- 8 trout fillets, boneless
- 1 cup farro
- Juice of 2 lemons
- Salt and black pepper to taste
- 1 avocado, chopped
- ¼ cup balsamic vinegar
- 1 garlic cloves, minced
- ¼ cup parsley, chopped
- ¼ cup mint, chopped
- 2 tbsp yellow mustard

Directions:

1. Boil salted water in a pot over medium heat and stir in farro. Simmer for 30 minutes and drain. Remove to a bowl and combine with lemon juice, mustard, garlic, salt, pepper, and half olive oil. Set aside. Mash the avocado with a fork in a bowl and mix with vinegar, salt, pepper, parsley, and mint.

2. Warm the remaining oil in a skillet over medium heat and brown trout fillets skin-side down for 10 minutes on both sides. Let cool and cut into pieces. Put over farro and stir in avocado dressing. Serve immediately.

Nutrition Info:

- Info Per Serving: Calories: 290;Fat: 13g;Protein: 37g;Carbs: 6g.

Shrimp & Spinach A La Puttanesca

Servings:4

Cooking Time:20 Minutes

Ingredients:

- 1 lb fresh shrimp, shells and tails removed
- 1 cup baby spinach
- 16 oz cooked spaghetti
- 2 tbsp olive oil
- 3 anchovy fillets, chopped
- 3 garlic cloves, minced
- ½ tsp crushed red pepper
- 1 can tomatoes, diced
- 12 black olives, sliced
- 2 tbsp capers
- 1 tsp dried oregano

Directions:

1. Warm the olive oil in a large skillet over medium heat. Add in the anchovies, garlic, and crushed red peppers and cook for 3 minutes, stirring frequently and mashing up the anchovies with a wooden spoon until they have melted into the oil. Pour in the tomatoes with their juices, olives, capers, and oregano. Simmer until the sauce is lightly bubbling, about 3-4 minutes. Stir in the shrimp. Cook for 6-8 minutes or until they turn pink and white, stirring occasionally. Add the baby spinach and spaghetti and stir for 2 minutes until the spinach wilts. Serve and enjoy!

Nutrition Info:

- Info Per Serving: Calories: 362;Fat: 13g;Protein: 30g;Carbs: 31g.

Crispy Herb Crusted Halibut

Servings:4

Cooking Time: 20 Minutes

Ingredients:

- 4 halibut fillets, patted dry
- Extra-virgin olive oil, for brushing
- ½ cup coarsely ground unsalted pistachios
- 1 tablespoon chopped fresh parsley
- 1 teaspoon chopped fresh basil
- 1 teaspoon chopped fresh thyme
- Pinch sea salt
- Pinch freshly ground black pepper

Directions:

1. Preheat the oven to 350ºF. Line a baking sheet with parchment paper.
2. Place the fillets on the baking sheet and brush them generously with olive oil.
3. In a small bowl, stir together the pistachios, parsley, basil, thyme, salt, and pepper.
4. Spoon the nut mixture evenly on the fish, spreading it out so the tops of the fillets are covered.
5. Bake in the preheated oven until it flakes when pressed with a fork, about 20 minutes.
6. Serve immediately.

Nutrition Info:

- Info Per Serving: Calories: 262;Fat: 11.0g;Protein: 32.0g;Carbs: 4.0g.

Andalusian Prawns With Capers

Servings:4

Cooking Time:25 Minutes

Ingredients:

- 1 lb prawns, peeled, deveined
- 2 tbsp olive oil
- 1 lemon, zested and juiced
- 2 tomatoes, chopped
- 1 cup spring onions, chopped
- 2 tbsp capers, chopped
- 2 tbsp dill, chopped
- Salt and black pepper to taste

Directions:

1. Warm the olive oil in a skillet over medium heat and cook onions and capers for 2-3 minutes. Stir in prawns, lemon zest, tomatoes, dill, salt, and pepper and cook for another 6 minutes. Serve drizzled with lemon juice.

Nutrition Info:

- Info Per Serving: Calories: 230;Fat: 14g;Protein: 6g;Carbs: 23g.

Caper & Squid Stew

Servings:4

Cooking Time:25 Minutes

Ingredients:

- 2 tbsp olive oil
- 1 onion, chopped
- 1 celery stalk, chopped
- 1 lb calamari rings
- 2 red chili peppers, chopped
- 2 garlic cloves, minced
- 14 oz canned tomatoes, diced
- 2 tbsp tomato paste
- Salt and black pepper to taste
- 2 tbsp capers, drained
- 12 black olives, pitted and halved

Directions:

1. Warm the olive oil in a skillet over medium heat and cook onion, celery, garlic, and chili peppers for 2 minutes. Stir in calamari rings, tomatoes, tomato paste, salt, and pepper and bring to a simmer. Cook for 20 minutes. Put in olives and capers and cook for another 5 minutes. Serve right away.

Nutrition Info:

- Info Per Serving: Calories: 280;Fat: 12g;Protein: 16g;Carbs: 14g.

Fried Scallops With Bean Mash

Servings:2

Cooking Time:20 Minutes

Ingredients:

- 4 tbsp olive oil
- 2 garlic cloves
- 2 tsp fresh thyme, minced
- 1 can cannellini beans
- ½ cup chicken stock
- Salt and black pepper to taste
- 10 oz sea scallops

Directions:

1. Warm 2 tablespoons of olive oil in a saucepan over medium heat. Sauté the garlic for 30 seconds or just until it's fragrant. Stir in the beans and stock and bring to a boil. Simmer for 5 minutes. Remove the beans to a bowl and mash them with a potato mash. Season with thyme, salt, and pepper.

2. Warm the remaining oil in a large sauté pan. Add the scallops, flat-side down, and cook for 2 minutes or until they're golden on the bottom. Flip over and cook for another 1-2 minutes or until opaque and slightly firm. Divide the bean mash between plates and top with scallops.

Nutrition Info:

- Info Per Serving: Calories: 465;Fat: 29g;Protein: 30g;Carbs: 21g.

Grilled Sardines With Herby Sauce

Servings:4

Cooking Time:15 Min + Marinating Time

Ingredients:

- 12 sardines, gutted and cleaned
- 1 lemon, cut into wedges
- 2 garlic cloves, minced
- 2 tbsp capers, finely chopped
- 1 tbsp whole capers
- 1 shallot, diced
- 1 tsp anchovy paste
- 1 lemon, zested and juiced
- 2 tbsp olive oil
- 1 tbsp parsley, finely chopped
- 1 tbsp basil, finely chopped

Directions:

1. In a bowl, blend garlic, chopped capers, shallot, anchovy paste, lemon zest, and olive oil. Add the sardines and toss to coat; let them sit to marinate for about 30 minutes.

2. Preheat your grill to high. Place the sardines on the grill. Cook for 3-4 minutes per side until the skin is browned and beginning to blister. Pour the marinade in a saucepan over medium heat and add the whole capers, parsley, basil, and lemon juice. Cook for 2-3 minutes until thickens. Pour the sauce over grilled sardines. Serve with lemon wedges.

Nutrition Info:

- Info Per Serving: Calories: 395;Fat: 21g;Protein: 46g;Carbs: 2.1g.

Lemony Trout With Caramelized Shallots

Servings:2

Cooking Time: 20 Minutes

Ingredients:

- Shallots:
- 1 teaspoon almond butter
- 2 shallots, thinly sliced
- Dash salt
- Trout:
- 1 tablespoon plus 1 teaspoon almond butter, divided
- 2 trout fillets
- 3 tablespoons capers
- ¼ cup freshly squeezed lemon juice
- ¼ teaspoon salt
- Dash freshly ground black pepper
- 1 lemon, thinly sliced

Directions:

1. Make the Shallots

2. In a large skillet over medium heat, cook the butter, shallots, and salt for 20 minutes, stirring every 5 minutes, or until the shallots are wilted and caramelized.

3. Make the Trout

4. Meanwhile, in another large skillet over medium heat, heat 1 teaspoon of almond butter.

5. Add the trout fillets and cook each side for 3 minutes, or until flaky. Transfer to a plate and set aside.

6. In the skillet used for the trout, stir in the capers, lemon juice, salt, and pepper, then bring to a simmer. Whisk in the remaining 1 tablespoon of almond butter. Spoon the sauce over the fish.

7. Garnish the fish with the lemon slices and caramelized shallots before serving.

Nutrition Info:

- Info Per Serving: Calories: 344;Fat: 18.4g;Protein: 21.1g;Carbs: 14.7g.

Honey-mustard Roasted Salmon

Servings:4

Cooking Time: 15 To 20 Minutes

Ingredients:

- 2 tablespoons whole-grain mustard
- 2 garlic cloves, minced
- 1 tablespoon honey
- ¼ teaspoon salt
- ¼ teaspoon freshly ground black pepper
- 1 pound salmon fillet
- Nonstick cooking spray

Directions:

1. Preheat the oven to 425ºF. Coat a baking sheet with nonstick cooking spray.
2. Stir together the mustard, garlic, honey, salt, and pepper in a small bowl.
3. Arrange the salmon fillet, skin-side down, on the coated baking sheet. Spread the mustard mixture evenly over the salmon fillet.
4. Roast in the preheated oven for 15 to 20 minutes, or until it flakes apart easily and reaches an internal temperature of 145ºF.
5. Serve hot.

Nutrition Info:

- Info Per Serving: Calories: 185;Fat: 7.0g;Protein: 23.2g;Carbs: 5.8g.

Parsley Salmon Bake

Servings:4

Cooking Time:20 Minutes

Ingredients:

- 2 tbsp olive oil
- 1 lb salmon fillets
- ¼ fresh parsley, chopped
- 1 garlic clove, minced
- ¼ tsp dried dill
- ¼ tsp chili powder
- ¼ tsp garlic powder
- 1 lemon, grated
- Salt and black pepper to taste

Directions:

1. Preheat oven to 350 F. Sprinkle the salmon with dill, chili powder, garlic powder, salt, and pepper.
2. Warm olive oil in a pan over medium heat and sear salmon skin-side down for 5 minutes. Transfer to the oven and bake for another 4-5 minutes. Combine parsley, lemon zest, garlic, and salt in a bowl. Serve salmon topped with the mixture.

Nutrition Info:

- Info Per Serving: Calories: 212;Fat: 14g;Protein: 22g;Carbs: 0.5g.

10-minute Cod With Parsley Pistou

Servings:4

Cooking Time: 10 Minutes

Ingredients:

- 1 cup packed roughly chopped fresh flat-leaf Italian parsley
- Zest and juice of 1 lemon
- 1 to 2 small garlic cloves, minced
- 1 teaspoon salt
- ½ teaspoon freshly ground black pepper
- 1 cup extra-virgin olive oil, divided
- 1 pound cod fillets, cut into 4 equal-sized pieces

Directions:

1. Make the pistou: Place the parsley, lemon zest and juice, garlic, salt, and pepper in a food processor until finely chopped.
2. With the food processor running, slowly drizzle in ¾ cup of olive oil until a thick sauce forms. Set aside.
3. Heat the remaining ¼ cup of olive oil in a large skillet over medium-high heat.
4. Add the cod fillets, cover, and cook each side for 4 to 5 minutes, until browned and cooked through.
5. Remove the cod fillets from the heat to a plate and top each with generous spoonfuls of the prepared pistou. Serve immediately.

Nutrition Info:

- Info Per Serving: Calories: 580;Fat: 54.6g;Protein: 21.1g;Carbs: 2.8g.

Mediterranean Grilled Sea Bass

Servings:6

Cooking Time: 20 Minutes

Ingredients:

- ¼ teaspoon onion powder
- ¼ teaspoon garlic powder
- ¼ teaspoon paprika
- Lemon pepper and sea salt to taste
- 2 pounds sea bass
- 3 tablespoons extra-virgin olive oil, divided
- 2 large cloves garlic, chopped
- 1 tablespoon chopped Italian flat leaf parsley

Directions:

1. Preheat the grill to high heat.
2. Place the onion powder, garlic powder, paprika, lemon pepper, and sea salt in a large bowl and stir to combine.
3. Dredge the fish in the spice mixture, turning until well coated.
4. Heat 2 tablespoon of olive oil in a small skillet. Add the garlic and parsley and cook for 1 to 2 minutes, stirring occasionally. Remove the skillet from the heat and set aside.
5. Brush the grill grates lightly with remaining 1 tablespoon olive oil.
6. Grill the fish for about 7 minutes. Flip the fish and drizzle with the garlic mixture and cook for an additional 7 minutes, or until the fish flakes when pressed lightly with a fork.
7. Serve hot.

Nutrition Info:

- Info Per Serving: Calories: 200;Fat: 10.3g;Protein: 26.9g;Carbs: 0.6g.

Seafood Cakes With Radicchio Salad

Servings:4

Cooking Time:30 Minutes

Ingredients:

- 2 tbsp butter
- 2 tbsp extra-virgin olive oil
- 1 lb lump crabmeat
- 4 scallions, sliced
- 1 garlic clove, minced
- ¼ cup cooked shrimp
- 2 tbsp heavy cream
- ¼ head radicchio, thinly sliced
- 1 green apple, shredded
- 2 tbsp lemon juice
- Salt and black pepper to taste

Directions:

1. In a food processor, place the shrimp, heavy cream, salt, and pepper. Blend until smooth. Mix crab meat and scallions in a bowl. Add in shrimp mixture and toss to combine. Make 4 patties out of the mixture. Transfer to the fridge for 10 minutes. Warm butter in a skillet over medium heat and brown patties for 8 minutes on all sides. Remove to a serving plate. Mix radicchio and apple in a bowl. Combine olive oil, lemon juice, garlic, and salt in a small bowl and stir well. Pour over the salad and toss to combine. Serve and enjoy!

Nutrition Info:

- Info Per Serving: Calories: 238;Fat: 14.3g;Protein: 20g;Carbs: 8g.

Dill Baked Sea Bass

Servings:6

Cooking Time: 10 To 15 Minutes

Ingredients:

- ¼ cup olive oil
- 2 pounds sea bass
- Sea salt and freshly ground pepper, to taste
- 1 garlic clove, minced
- ¼ cup dry white wine
- 3 teaspoons fresh dill
- 2 teaspoons fresh thyme

Directions:

1. Preheat the oven to 425°F.
2. Brush the bottom of a roasting pan with the olive oil. Place the fish in the pan and brush the fish with oil.
3. Season the fish with sea salt and freshly ground pepper. Combine the remaining ingredients and pour over the fish.
4. Bake in the preheated oven for 10 to 15 minutes, depending on the size of the fish.
5. Serve hot.

Nutrition Info:

- Info Per Serving: Calories: 224;Fat: 12.1g;Protein: 28.1g;Carbs: 0.9g.

Shrimp & Salmon In Tomato Sauce

Servings:4

Cooking Time:30 Minutes

Ingredients:

- 1 lb shrimp, peeled and deveined
- 2 tbsp olive oil
- 1 lb salmon fillets
- Salt and black pepper to taste
- 1 cups tomatoes, chopped
- 1 onion, chopped
- 2 garlic cloves, minced
- ¼ tsp red pepper flakes
- 1 cup fish stock
- 1 tbsp cilantro, chopped

Directions:

1. Preheat the oven to 360F. Line a baking sheet with parchment paper. Season the salmon with salt and pepper, drizzle with some olive oil, and arrange them on the sheet. Bake for 15 minutes. Remove to a serving plate.

2. Warm the remaining olive oil in a skillet over medium heat and sauté onion and garlic for 3 minutes until tender. Pour in tomatoes, fish stock, salt, pepper, and red pepper flakes and bring to a boil. Simmer for 10 minutes. Stir in shrimp and cook for another 8 minutes. Pour the sauce over the salmon and serve sprinkled with cilantro.

Nutrition Info:

- Info Per Serving: Calories: 240;Fat: 16g;Protein: 18g;Carbs: 22g.

Lemon Rosemary Roasted Branzino

Servings:2

Cooking Time: 30 Minutes

Ingredients:

- 4 tablespoons extra-virgin olive oil, divided
- 2 branzino fillets, preferably at least 1 inch thick
- 1 garlic clove, minced
- 1 bunch scallions (white part only), thinly sliced
- 10 to 12 small cherry tomatoes, halved
- 1 large carrot, cut into ¼-inch rounds
- ½ cup dry white wine
- 2 tablespoons paprika
- 2 teaspoons kosher salt
- ½ tablespoon ground chili pepper
- 2 rosemary sprigs or 1 tablespoon dried rosemary
- 1 small lemon, thinly sliced
- ½ cup sliced pitted kalamata olives

Directions:

1. Heat a large ovenproof skillet over high heat until hot, about 2 minutes. Add 1 tablespoon of olive oil and heat for 10 to 15 seconds until it shimmers.

2. Add the branzino fillets, skin-side up, and sear for 2 minutes. Flip the fillets and cook for an additional 2 minutes. Set aside.

3. Swirl 2 tablespoons of olive oil around the skillet to coat evenly.

4. Add the garlic, scallions, tomatoes, and carrot, and sauté for 5 minutes, or until softened.

5. Add the wine, stirring until all ingredients are well combined. Carefully place the fish over the sauce.

6. Preheat the oven to 450ºF.

7. Brush the fillets with the remaining 1 tablespoon of olive oil and season with paprika, salt, and chili pepper. Top each fillet with a rosemary sprig and lemon slices. Scatter the olives over fish and around the skillet.

8. Roast for about 10 minutes until the lemon slices are browned. Serve hot.

Nutrition Info:

- Info Per Serving: Calories: 724;Fat: 43.0g;Protein: 57.7g;Carbs: 25.0g.

Balsamic-honey Glazed Salmon

Servings:4

Cooking Time: 8 Minutes

Ingredients:

- ½ cup balsamic vinegar
- 1 tablespoon honey
- 4 salmon fillets
- Sea salt and freshly ground pepper, to taste
- 1 tablespoon olive oil

Directions:

1. Heat a skillet over medium-high heat. Combine the vinegar and honey in a small bowl.

2. Season the salmon fillets with the sea salt and freshly ground pepper; brush with the honey-balsamic glaze.

3. Add olive oil to the skillet, and sear the salmon fillets, cooking for 3 to 4 minutes on each side until lightly browned and medium rare in the center.

4. Let sit for 5 minutes before serving.

Nutrition Info:

- Info Per Serving: Calories: 454;Fat: 17.3g;Protein: 65.3g;Carbs: 9.7g.

Spicy Cod Fillets

Servings:4
Cooking Time:35 Minutes

Ingredients:

- 2 tbsp olive oil
- 1 tsp lime juice
- Salt and black pepper to taste
- 1 tsp sweet paprika
- 1 tsp chili powder
- 1 onion, chopped
- 2 garlic cloves, minced
- 4 cod fillets, boneless
- 1 tsp ground coriander
- ½ cup fish stock
- ½ lb cherry tomatoes, cubed

Directions:

1. Warm olive oil in a skillet over medium heat. Season the cod with salt, pepper, and chili powder and cook in the skillet for 8 minutes on all sides; set aside. In the same skillet, cook onion and garlic for 3 minutes. Stir in lime juice, paprika, coriander, fish stock, and cherry tomatoes and bring to a boil. Simmer for 10 minutes. Serve topped with cod fillets.

Nutrition Info:

- Info Per Serving: Calories: 240;Fat: 17g;Protein: 17g;Carbs: 26g.

Oven-baked Spanish Salmon

Servings:4
Cooking Time:30 Minutes

Ingredients:

- 15 green pimiento-stuffed olives
- 2 small red onions, sliced
- 1 cup fennel bulbs shaved
- 1 cup cherry tomatoes
- Salt and black pepper to taste
- 1 tsp cumin seeds
- ½ tsp smoked paprika
- 4 salmon fillets
- ½ cup chicken broth
- 3 tbsp olive oil
- 2 cups cooked farro

Directions:

1. Preheat oven to 375 F. In a bowl, combine the onions, fennel, tomatoes, and olives. Season with salt, pepper, cumin, and paprika and mix well. Spread out on a greased baking dish. Arrange the fish fillets over the vegetables, season with salt, and gently pour the broth over. Drizzle with olive oil and bake for 20 minutes. Serve over farro.

Nutrition Info:

- Info Per Serving: Calories: 475;Fat: 18g;Protein: 50g;Carbs: 26g.

Vegetable Mains And Meatless Recipes

Simple Honey-glazed Baby Carrots

Servings:2
Cooking Time: 6 Minutes

Ingredients:

- ⅔ cup water
- 1½ pounds baby carrots
- 4 tablespoons almond butter
- ½ cup honey
- 1 teaspoon dried thyme
- 1½ teaspoons dried dill
- Salt, to taste

Directions:

1. Pour the water into the Instant Pot and add a steamer basket. Place the baby carrots in the basket.
2. Secure the lid. Select the Manual mode and set the cooking time for 4 minutes at High Pressure.
3. Once cooking is complete, do a quick pressure release. Carefully open the lid.
4. Transfer the carrots to a plate and set aside.
5. Pour the water out of the Instant Pot and dry it.
6. Press the Sauté button on the Instant Pot and heat the almond butter.
7. Stir in the honey, thyme, and dill.
8. Return the carrots to the Instant Pot and stir until well coated. Sauté for another 1 minute.
9. Taste and season with salt as needed. Serve warm.

Nutrition Info:

- Info Per Serving: Calories: 575;Fat: 23.5g;Protein: 2.8g;Carbs: 90.6g.

Sweet Mustard Cabbage Hash

Servings:4
Cooking Time:30 Minutes

Ingredients:

- 1 head Savoy cabbage, shredded
- 3 tbsp olive oil
- 1 onion, finely chopped
- 2 garlic cloves, minced
- ½ tsp fennel seeds
- ¼ cup red wine vinegar
- 1 tbsp mustard powder
- 1 tbsp honey
- Salt and black pepper to taste

Directions:

1. Warm olive oil in a pan over medium heat and sauté onion, fennel seeds, cabbage, salt, and pepper for 8-9 minutes.
2. In a bowl, mix vinegar, mustard, and honey; set aside. Sauté garlic in the pan for 30 seconds. Pour in vinegar mixture and cook for 10-15 minutes until the liquid reduces by half.

Nutrition Info:

- Info Per Serving: Calories: 181;Fat: 12g;Protein: 3.4g;Carbs: 19g.

Minty Broccoli & Walnuts

Servings:2
Cooking Time:10 Minutes

Ingredients:

- 1 garlic clove, minced
- ½ cups walnuts, chopped
- 3 cups broccoli florets, steamed
- 1 tbsp mint, chopped
- ½ lemon, juiced
- Salt and black pepper to taste

Directions:

1. Mix walnuts, broccoli, garlic, mint, lemon juice, salt, and pepper in a bowl. Serve chilled.

Nutrition Info:

- Info Per Serving: Calories: 210;Fat: 7g;Protein: 4g;Carbs: 9g.

Balsamic Grilled Vegetables

Servings:4
Cooking Time:20 Minutes

Ingredients:

- ¼ cup olive oil
- 4 carrots, cut in half
- 2 onions, quartered
- 1 zucchini, cut into rounds
- 1 eggplant, cut into rounds
- 1 red bell pepper, chopped
- Salt and black pepper to taste
- Balsamic vinegar to taste

Directions:

1. Heat your grill to medium-high. Brush the vegetables lightly with olive oil, and season with salt and pepper. Grill the vegetables for 3–4 minutes per side. Transfer to a serving dish and drizzle with balsamic vinegar. Serve and enjoy!

Nutrition Info:

- Info Per Serving: Calories: 184;Fat: 14g;Protein: 2.1g;Carbs: 14g.

Fried Eggplant Rolls

Servings:4
Cooking Time: 10 Minutes

Ingredients:

- 2 large eggplants, trimmed and cut lengthwise into ¼-inch-thick slices
- 1 teaspoon salt
- 1 cup shredded ricotta cheese
- 4 ounces goat cheese, shredded
- ¼ cup finely chopped fresh basil
- ½ teaspoon freshly ground black pepper
- Olive oil spray

Directions:

1. Add the eggplant slices to a colander and season with salt. Set aside for 15 to 20 minutes.
2. Mix together the ricotta and goat cheese, basil, and black pepper in a large bowl and stir to combine. Set aside.
3. Dry the eggplant slices with paper towels and lightly mist them with olive oil spray.
4. Heat a large skillet over medium heat and lightly spray it with olive oil spray.
5. Arrange the eggplant slices in the skillet and fry each side for 3 minutes until golden brown.
6. Remove from the heat to a paper towel-lined plate and rest for 5 minutes.
7. Make the eggplant rolls: Lay the eggplant slices on a flat work surface and top each slice with a tablespoon of the prepared cheese mixture. Roll them up and serve immediately.

Nutrition Info:

- Info Per Serving: Calories: 254;Fat: 14.9g;Protein: 15.3g;Carbs: 18.6g.

Grilled Romaine Lettuce

Servings:4

Cooking Time: 3 To 5 Minutes

Ingredients:

- Romaine:
- 2 heads romaine lettuce, halved lengthwise
- 2 tablespoons extra-virgin olive oil
- Dressing:
- ½ cup unsweetened almond milk
- 1 tablespoon extra-virgin olive oil
- ¼ bunch fresh chives, thinly chopped
- 1 garlic clove, pressed
- 1 pinch red pepper flakes

Directions:

1. Heat a grill pan over medium heat.

2. Brush each lettuce half with the olive oil. Place the lettuce halves, flat-side down, on the grill. Grill for 3 to 5 minutes, or until the lettuce slightly wilts and develops light grill marks.

3. Meanwhile, whisk together all the ingredients for the dressing in a small bowl.

4. Drizzle 2 tablespoons of the dressing over each romaine half and serve.

Nutrition Info:

- Info Per Serving: Calories: 126;Fat: 11.0g;Protein: 2.0g;Carbs: 7.0g.

5-ingredient Zucchini Fritters

Servings:14

Cooking Time: 5 Minutes

Ingredients:

- 4 cups grated zucchini
- Salt, to taste
- 2 large eggs, lightly beaten
- ⅓ cup sliced scallions (green and white parts)
- ⅔ all-purpose flour
- ⅛ teaspoon black pepper
- 2 tablespoons olive oil

Directions:

1. Put the grated zucchini in a colander and lightly season with salt. Set aside to rest for 10 minutes. Squeeze out as much liquid from the grated zucchini as possible.

2. Pour the grated zucchini into a bowl. Fold in the beaten eggs, scallions, flour, salt, and pepper and stir until everything is well combined.

3. Heat the olive oil in a large skillet over medium heat until hot.

4. Drop 3 tablespoons mounds of the zucchini mixture onto the hot skillet to make each fritter, pressing them lightly into rounds and spacing them about 2 inches apart.

5. Cook for 2 to 3 minutes. Flip the zucchini fritters and cook for 2 minutes more, or until they are golden brown and cooked through.

6. Remove from the heat to a plate lined with paper towels. Repeat with the remaining zucchini mixture.

7. Serve hot.

Nutrition Info:

- Info Per Serving: Calories: 113;Fat: 6.1g;Protein: 4.0g;Carbs: 12.2g.

Creamy Cauliflower Chickpea Curry

Servings:4

Cooking Time: 15 Minutes

Ingredients:

- 3 cups fresh or frozen cauliflower florets
- 2 cups unsweetened almond milk
- 1 can low-sodium chickpeas, drained and rinsed
- 1 can coconut milk
- 1 tablespoon curry powder
- ¼ teaspoon garlic powder
- ¼ teaspoon ground ginger
- ⅛ teaspoon onion powder
- ¼ teaspoon salt

Directions:

1. Add the cauliflower florets, almond milk, chickpeas, coconut milk, curry powder, garlic powder, ginger, and onion powder to a large stockpot and stir to combine.
2. Cover and cook over medium-high heat for 10 minutes, stirring occasionally.
3. Reduce the heat to low and continue cooking uncovered for 5 minutes, or until the cauliflower is tender.
4. Sprinkle with the salt and stir well. Serve warm.

Nutrition Info:

- Info Per Serving: Calories: 409;Fat: 29.6g;Protein: 10.0g;Carbs: 29.8g.

Steamed Beetroot With Nutty Yogurt

Servings:4

Cooking Time:30 Min + Chilling Time

Ingredients:

- ¼ cup extra virgin olive oil
- 1 lb beetroots, cut into wedges
- 1 cup Greek yogurt
- 3 spring onions, sliced
- 5 dill pickles, finely chopped
- 2 garlic cloves, minced
- 2 tbsp fresh parsley, chopped
- 1 oz mixed nuts, crushed
- Salt to taste

Directions:

1. In a pot over medium heat, insert a steamer basket and pour in 1 cup of water. Place in the beetroots and steam for 10-15 minutes until tender. Remove to a plate and let cool. In a bowl, combine the pickles, spring onions, garlic, salt, 3 tbsp of olive oil, Greek yogurt, and nuts and mix well. Spread the yogurt mixture on a serving plate and arrange the beetroot wedges on top. Drizzle with the remaining olive oil and top with parsley. Serve and enjoy!

Nutrition Info:

- Info Per Serving: Calories: 271;Fat: 18g;Protein: 9.6g;Carbs: 22g.

Roasted Celery Root With Yogurt Sauce

Servings:6
Cooking Time:50 Minutes
Ingredients:

- 3 tbsp olive oil
- 3 celery roots, sliced
- Salt and black pepper to taste
- ¼ cup plain yogurt
- ¼ tsp grated lemon zest
- 1 tsp lemon juice
- 1 tsp sesame seeds, toasted
- 1 tsp coriander seeds, crushed
- ¼ tsp dried thyme
- ¼ tsp chili powder
- ¼ cup fresh cilantro, chopped

Directions:

1. Preheat oven to 425 F. Place the celery slices on a baking sheet. Sprinkle them with olive oil, salt, and pepper. Roast for 25-30 minutes. Flip each piece and continue to roast for 10-15 minutes until celery root is very tender and sides touching sheet are browned. Transfer celery to a serving platter.
2. Whisk yogurt, lemon zest and juice, and salt together in a bowl. In a separate bowl, combine sesame seeds, coriander seeds, thyme, chili powder, and salt. Drizzle celery root with yogurt sauce and sprinkle with seed mixture and cilantro.

Nutrition Info:

- Info Per Serving: Calories: 75;Fat: 7.5g;Protein: 0.7g;Carbs: 1.8g.

Spanish-style Green Beans With Pine Nuts

Servings:6
Cooking Time:30 Minutes
Ingredients:

- ¼ cup Manchego cheese, shredded
- ¼ cup olive oil
- 2 lb green beans, trimmed
- Salt and black pepper to taste
- 2 garlic cloves, minced
- 1 tsp Dijon mustard
- 2 tbsp fresh parsley, chopped
- 2 tbsp pine nuts, toasted

Directions:

1. Preheat oven to 420 F. Toss green beans with some olive oil, salt, and pepper. Transfer to a baking sheet and roast for 15-18 minutes, shaking occasionally the sheet. Transfer green beans to a serving plate. Microwave mixed garlic, lemon zest, salt, pepper, and the remaining olive oil for about 1 minute until bubbling. Let the mixture sit for 1 minute, then whisk in lemon juice, mustard, salt, and pepper. Drizzle the green beans with the dressing and sprinkle with basil. Top with cheese and pine nuts. Serve and enjoy!

Nutrition Info:

- Info Per Serving: Calories: 126;Fat: 11g;Protein: 2.6g;Carbs: 6.3g.

Tradicional Matchuba Green Beans

Servings:4
Cooking Time:15 Minutes
Ingredients:

- 1 ¼ lb narrow green beans, trimmed
- 3 tbsp butter, melted
- 1 cup Moroccan matbucha
- 2 green onions, chopped
- Salt and black pepper to taste

Directions:

1. Steam the green beans in a pot for 5-6 minutes until tender. Remove to a bowl, reserving the cooking liquid. In a skillet over medium heat, melt the butter. Add in green onions, salt, and black pepper and cook until fragrant. Lower the heat and put in the green beans along with some of the reserved water. Simmer for 3-4 minutes. Serve the green beans with the Sabra Moroccan matbucha as a dip.

Nutrition Info:

- Info Per Serving: Calories: 125;Fat: 8.6g;Protein: 2.2g;Carbs: 9g.

Baked Tomatoes And Chickpeas

Servings:4

Cooking Time: 40 To 45 Minutes

Ingredients:

- 1 tablespoon extra-virgin olive oil
- ½ medium onion, chopped
- 3 garlic cloves, chopped
- ¼ teaspoon ground cumin
- 2 teaspoons smoked paprika
- 2 cans chickpeas, drained and rinsed
- 4 cups halved cherry tomatoes
- ½ cup plain Greek yogurt, for serving
- 1 cup crumbled feta cheese, for serving

Directions:

1. Preheat the oven to 425°F.
2. Heat the olive oil in an ovenproof skillet over medium heat.
3. Add the onion and garlic and sauté for about 5 minutes, stirring occasionally, or until tender and fragrant.
4. Add the paprika and cumin and cook for 2 minutes. Stir in the chickpeas and tomatoes and allow to simmer for 5 to 10 minutes.
5. Transfer the skillet to the preheated oven and roast for 25 to 30 minutes, or until the mixture bubbles and thickens.
6. Remove from the oven and serve topped with yogurt and crumbled feta cheese.

Nutrition Info:

- Info Per Serving: Calories: 411;Fat: 14.9g;Protein: 20.2g;Carbs: 50.7g.

Spicy Roasted Tomatoes

Servings:2

Cooking Time:50 Minutes

Ingredients:

- ¼ cup olive oil
- 1 lb mixed cherry tomatoes
- 10 garlic cloves, minced
- Salt to taste
- 1 fresh rosemary sprig
- 1 fresh thyme sprig
- 2 crusty bread slices

Directions:

1. Preheat oven to 350 F. Toss the cherry tomatoes, garlic, olive oil, and salt in a baking dish. Top with the herb sprigs. Roast the tomatoes for about 45 minutes until they are soft and begin to caramelize. Discard the herbs and serve with bread.

Nutrition Info:

- Info Per Serving: Calories: 271;Fat: 26g;Protein: 3g;Carbs: 12g.

Parmesan Asparagus With Tomatoes

Servings:6

Cooking Time:30 Minutes

Ingredients:

- 3 tbsp olive oil
- 2 garlic cloves, minced
- 12 oz cherry tomatoes, halved
- 1 tsp dried oregano
- 10 Kalamata olives, chopped
- 2 lb asparagus, trimmed
- 2 tbsp fresh basil, chopped
- ¼ cup Parmesan cheese, grated
- Salt and black pepper to taste

Directions:

1. Warm 2 tbsp of olive oil in a skillet over medium heat sauté the garlic for 1-2 minutes, stirring often, until golden. Add tomatoes, olives, and oregano and cook until tomatoes begin to break down, about 3 minutes; transfer to a bowl.
2. Coat the asparagus with the remaining olive oil and cook in a grill pan over medium heat for about 5 minutes, turning once until crisp-tender. Sprinkle with salt and pepper. Transfer asparagus to a serving platter, top with tomato mixture, and sprinkle with basil and Parmesan cheese. Serve and enjoy!

Nutrition Info:

- Info Per Serving: Calories: 157;Fat: 7g;Protein: 7.3g;Carbs: 19g.

Butternut Noodles With Mushrooms

Servings:4

Cooking Time: 12 Minutes

Ingredients:

- ¼ cup extra-virgin olive oil
- 1 pound cremini mushrooms, sliced
- ½ red onion, finely chopped
- 1 teaspoon dried thyme
- ½ teaspoon sea salt
- 3 garlic cloves, minced
- ½ cup dry white wine
- Pinch of red pepper flakes
- 4 cups butternut noodles
- 4 ounces grated Parmesan cheese

Directions:

1. In a large skillet over medium-high heat, heat the olive oil until shimmering. Add the mushrooms, onion, thyme, and salt to the skillet. Cook for about 6 minutes, stirring occasionally, or until the mushrooms start to brown. Add the garlic and sauté for 30 seconds. Stir in the white wine and red pepper flakes.
2. Fold in the noodles. Cook for about 5 minutes, stirring occasionally, or until the noodles are tender.
3. Serve topped with the grated Parmesan.

Nutrition Info:

- Info Per Serving: Calories: 244;Fat: 14.0g;Protein: 4.0g;Carbs: 22.0g.

Quick Steamed Broccoli

Servings:2

Cooking Time: 0 Minutes

Ingredients:

- ¼ cup water
- 3 cups broccoli florets
- Salt and ground black pepper, to taste

Directions:

1. Pour the water into the Instant Pot and insert a steamer basket. Place the broccoli florets in the basket.
2. Secure the lid. Select the Manual mode and set the cooking time for 0 minutes at High Pressure.
3. Once cooking is complete, do a quick pressure release. Carefully open the lid.
4. Transfer the broccoli florets to a bowl with cold water to keep bright green color.
5. Season the broccoli with salt and pepper to taste, then serve.

Nutrition Info:

- Info Per Serving: Calories: 16;Fat: 0.2g;Protein: 1.9g;Carbs: 1.7g.

Roasted Caramelized Root Vegetables

Servings:6

Cooking Time:40 Minutes

Ingredients:

- 1 sweet potato, peeled and cut into chunks
- 3 tbsp olive oil
- 2 carrots, peeled
- 2 beets, peeled
- 1 turnip, peeled
- 1 tsp cumin
- 1 tsp sweet paprika
- Salt and black pepper to taste
- 1 lemon, juiced
- 2 tbsp parsley, chopped

Directions:

1. Preheat oven to 400 F. Cut the vegetables into chunks and toss them with olive oil and seasonings in a sheet pan. Drizzle with lemon juice and roast them for 35-40 minutes until vegetables are tender and golden. Serve topped with parsley.

Nutrition Info:

- Info Per Serving: Calories: 80;Fat: 4.8g;Protein: 1.5g;Carbs: 8.9g.

Moroccan Tagine With Vegetables

Servings:2

Cooking Time: 40 Minutes

Ingredients:

- 2 tablespoons olive oil
- ½ onion, diced
- 1 garlic clove, minced
- 2 cups cauliflower florets
- 1 medium carrot, cut into 1-inch pieces
- 1 cup diced eggplant
- 1 can whole tomatoes with their juices
- 1 can chickpeas, drained and rinsed
- 2 small red potatoes, cut into 1-inch pieces
- 1 cup water
- 1 teaspoon pure maple syrup
- ½ teaspoon cinnamon
- ½ teaspoon turmeric
- 1 teaspoon cumin
- ½ teaspoon salt
- 1 to 2 teaspoons harissa paste

Directions:

1. In a Dutch oven, heat the olive oil over medium-high heat. Sauté the onion for 5 minutes, stirring occasionally, or until the onion is translucent.

2. Stir in the garlic, cauliflower florets, carrot, eggplant, tomatoes, and potatoes. Using a wooden spoon or spatula to break up the tomatoes into smaller pieces.

3. Add the chickpeas, water, maple syrup, cinnamon, turmeric, cumin, and salt and stir to incorporate. Bring the mixture to a boil.

4. Once it starts to boil, reduce the heat to medium-low. Stir in the harissa paste, cover, allow to simmer for about 40 minutes, or until the vegetables are softened. Taste and adjust seasoning as needed.

5. Let the mixture cool for 5 minutes before serving.

Nutrition Info:

- Info Per Serving: Calories: 293;Fat: 9.9g;Protein: 11.2g;Carbs: 45.5g.

Roasted Vegetables

Servings:2

Cooking Time: 35 Minutes

Ingredients:

- 6 teaspoons extra-virgin olive oil, divided
- 12 to 15 Brussels sprouts, halved
- 1 medium sweet potato, peeled and cut into 2-inch cubes
- 2 cups fresh cauliflower florets
- 1 medium zucchini, cut into 1-inch rounds
- 1 red bell pepper, cut into 1-inch slices
- Salt, to taste

Directions:

1. Preheat the oven to 425ºF.

2. Add 2 teaspoons of olive oil, Brussels sprouts, sweet potato, and salt to a large bowl and toss until they are completely coated.

3. Transfer them to a large roasting pan and roast for 10 minutes, or until the Brussels sprouts are lightly browned.

4. Meantime, combine the cauliflower florets with 2 teaspoons of olive oil and salt in a separate bowl.

5. Remove from the oven. Add the cauliflower florets to the roasting pan and roast for 10 minutes more.

6. Meanwhile, toss the zucchini and bell pepper with the remaining olive oil in a medium bowl until well coated. Season with salt.

7. Remove the roasting pan from the oven and stir in the zucchini and bell pepper. Continue roasting for 15 minutes, or until the vegetables are fork-tender.

8. Divide the roasted vegetables between two plates and serve warm.

Nutrition Info:

- Info Per Serving: Calories: 333;Fat: 16.8g;Protein: 12.2g;Carbs: 37.6g.

Spicy Potato Wedges

Servings:4

Cooking Time:30 Minutes

Ingredients:

- 1 ½ lb potatoes, peeled and cut into wedges
- 3 tbsp olive oil
- 1 tbsp minced fresh rosemary
- 2 tsp chili powder
- 3 garlic cloves, minced
- Salt and black pepper to taste

Directions:

1. Preheat the oven to 370 F. Toss the wedges with olive oil, garlic, salt, and pepper. Spread out in a roasting sheet. Roast for 15-20 minutes until browned and crisp at the edges. Remove and sprinkle with chili powder and rosemary.

Nutrition Info:

- Info Per Serving: Calories: 152;Fat: 7g;Protein: 2.5g;Carbs: 21g.

Parmesan Stuffed Zucchini Boats

Servings:4

Cooking Time: 15 Minutes

Ingredients:

- 1 cup canned low-sodium chickpeas, drained and rinsed
- 1 cup no-sugar-added spaghetti sauce
- 2 zucchinis
- ¼ cup shredded Parmesan cheese

Directions:

1. Preheat the oven to 425ºF.
2. In a medium bowl, stir together the chickpeas and spaghetti sauce.
3. Cut the zucchini in half lengthwise and scrape a spoon gently down the length of each half to remove the seeds.
4. Fill each zucchini half with the chickpea sauce and top with one-quarter of the Parmesan cheese.
5. Place the zucchini halves on a baking sheet and roast in the oven for 15 minutes.
6. Transfer to a plate. Let rest for 5 minutes before serving.

Nutrition Info:

- Info Per Serving: Calories: 139;Fat: 4.0g;Protein: 8.0g;Carbs: 20.0g.

Sweet Potato Chickpea Buddha Bowl

Servings:2
Cooking Time: 10 To 15 Minutes
Ingredients:

- Sauce:
- 1 tablespoon tahini
- 2 tablespoons plain Greek yogurt
- 2 tablespoons hemp seeds
- 1 garlic clove, minced
- Pinch salt

- Freshly ground black pepper, to taste
- Bowl:
- 1 small sweet potato, peeled and finely diced
- 1 teaspoon extra-virgin olive oil
- 1 cup from 1 can low-sodium chickpeas, drained and rinsed
- 2 cups baby kale

Directions:

1. Make the Sauce
2. Whisk together the tahini and yogurt in a small bowl.
3. Stir in the hemp seeds and minced garlic. Season with salt pepper. Add 2 to 3 tablespoons water to create a creamy yet pourable consistency and set aside.
4. Make the Bowl
5. Preheat the oven to 425°F. Line a baking sheet with parchment paper.
6. Place the sweet potato on the prepared baking sheet and drizzle with the olive oil. Toss well
7. Roast in the preheated oven for 10 to 15 minutes, stirring once during cooking, or until fork-tender and browned.
8. In each of 2 bowls, place ½ cup of chickpeas, 1 cup of baby kale, and half of the cooked sweet potato. Serve drizzled with half of the prepared sauce.

Nutrition Info:

- Info Per Serving: Calories: 323;Fat: 14.1g;Protein: 17.0g;Carbs: 36.0g.

Tomatoes Filled With Tabbouleh

Servings:4
Cooking Time:25 Minutes
Ingredients:

- 3 tbsp olive oil, divided
- 8 medium tomatoes
- ½ cup water
- ½ cup bulgur wheat
- 1 ½ cups minced parsley
- ⅓ cup minced fresh mint
- 2 scallions, chopped
- 1 tsp sumac
- Salt and black pepper to taste
- 1 lemon, zested

Directions:

1. Place the bulgur wheat and 2 cups of salted water in a pot and bring to a boil. Lower the heat and simmer for 10 minutes or until tender. Remove the pot from the heat and cover with a lid. Let it sit for 15 minutes.
2. Preheat the oven to 400 F. Slice off the top of each tomato and scoop out the pulp and seeds using a spoon into a sieve set over a bowl. Drain and discard any excess liquid; chop the remaining pulp and place it in a large mixing bowl. Add in parsley, mint, scallions, sumac, lemon zest, lemon juice, bulgur, pepper, and salt, and mix well.
3. Spoon the filling into the tomatoes and place the lids on top. Drizzle with olive oil and bake for 15-20 minutes until the tomatoes are tender. Serve and enjoy!

Nutrition Info:

- Info Per Serving: Calories: 160;Fat: 7g;Protein: 5g;Carbs: 22g.

Spinach & Lentil Stew

Servings:4

Cooking Time:40 Minutes

Ingredients:

- 2 tbsp olive oil
- 1 cup dry red lentils, rinsed
- 1 carrot, chopped
- 1 celery stalk, chopped
- 1 red onion, chopped
- 4 garlic cloves, minced
- 3 tomatoes, puréed
- 3 cups vegetable broth
- 1 tsp cayenne pepper
- ½ tsp ground cumin
- ½ tsp thyme
- 1 tsp turmeric
- 1 tbsp sweet paprika
- 1 cup spinach, chopped
- 1 cup fresh cilantro, chopped
- Salt and black pepper to taste

Directions:

1. Heat the olive oil in a pot over medium heat and sauté the garlic, carrot, celery, and onion until tender, about 4-5 minutes. Stir in cayenne pepper, cumin, thyme, paprika, and turmeric for 1 minute and add tomatoes; cook for 3 more minutes. Pour in vegetable broth and lentils and bring to a boil. Reduce the heat and simmer covered for 15 minutes. Stir in spinach and cook for 5 minutes until wilted. Adjust the seasoning and divide between bowls. Top with cilantro.

Nutrition Info:

- Info Per Serving: Calories: 310;Fat: 9g;Protein: 18.3g;Carbs: 41g.

Sautéed Cabbage With Parsley

Servings:4

Cooking Time: 12 To 14 Minutes

Ingredients:

- 1 small head green cabbage, cored and sliced thin
- 2 tablespoons extra-virgin olive oil, divided
- 1 onion, halved and sliced thin
- ¾ teaspoon salt, divided
- ¼ teaspoon black pepper
- ¼ cup chopped fresh parsley
- 1½ teaspoons lemon juice

Directions:

1. Place the cabbage in a large bowl with cold water. Let sit for 3 minutes. Drain well.

2. Heat 1 tablespoon of the oil in a skillet over medium-high heat until shimmering. Add the onion and ¼ teaspoon of the salt and cook for 5 to 7 minutes, or until softened and lightly browned. Transfer to a bowl.

3. Heat the remaining 1 tablespoon of the oil in now-empty skillet over medium-high heat until shimmering. Add the cabbage and sprinkle with the remaining ½ teaspoon of the salt and black pepper. Cover and cook for about 3 minutes, without stirring, or until cabbage is wilted and lightly browned on bottom.

4. Stir and continue to cook for about 4 minutes, uncovered, or until the cabbage is crisp-tender and lightly browned in places, stirring once halfway through cooking. Off heat, stir in the cooked onion, parsley and lemon juice.

5. Transfer to a plate and serve.

Nutrition Info:

- Info Per Serving: Calories: 117;Fat: 7.0g;Protein: 2.7g;Carbs: 13.4g.

Sides , Salads, And Soups Recipes

Cheese & Broccoli Quiche

Servings:4

Cooking Time:45 Minutes

Ingredients:

- 1 tsp Mediterranean seasoning
- 3 eggs
- ½ cup heavy cream
- 3 tbsp olive oil
- 1 red onion, chopped
- 2 garlic cloves, minced
- 2 oz mozzarella, shredded
- 1 lb broccoli, cut into florets

Directions:

1. Preheat oven to 320 F. Warm the oil in a pan over medium heat. Sauté the onion and garlic until just tender and fragrant. Add in the broccoli and continue to cook until crisp-tender for about 4 minutes. Spoon the mixture into a greased casserole dish. Beat the eggs with heavy cream and Mediterranean seasoning. Spoon this mixture over the broccoli layer. Bake for 18-20 minutes. Top with the shredded cheese and broil for 5 to 6 minutes or until hot and bubbly on the top. Serve.

Nutrition Info:

- Info Per Serving: Calories: 198;Fat: 14g;Protein: 5g;Carbs: 12g.

Avgolemono (lemon Chicken Soup)

Servings:2

Cooking Time: 60 Minutes

Ingredients:

- ½ large onion
- 2 medium carrots
- 1 celery stalk
- 1 garlic clove
- 5 cups low-sodium chicken stock
- ¼ cup brown rice
- 1½ cups shredded rotisserie chicken
- 3 tablespoons freshly squeezed lemon juice
- 1 egg yolk
- 2 tablespoons chopped fresh dill
- 2 tablespoons chopped fresh parsley
- Salt, to taste

Directions:

1. Put the onion, carrots, celery, and garlic in a food processor and pulse until the vegetables are minced.
2. Add the vegetables and chicken stock to a stockpot and bring it to a boil over high heat.
3. Reduce the heat to medium-low and add the rice, shredded chicken and lemon juice. Cover, and let the soup simmer for 40 minutes, or until the rice is cooked.
4. In a small bowl, whisk the egg yolk lightly. Slowly, while whisking with one hand, pour about ½ of a ladle of the broth into the egg yolk to warm, or temper, the yolk. Slowly add another ladle of broth and continue to whisk.
5. Remove the soup from the heat and pour the whisked egg yolk–broth mixture into the pot. Stir well to combine.
6. Add the fresh dill and parsley. Season with salt to taste and serve.

Nutrition Info:

- Info Per Serving: Calories: 172;Fat: 4.2g;Protein: 18.2g;Carbs: 16.1g.

Traditional Dukkah Spice

Servings:6

Cooking Time:50 Minutes

Ingredients:

- ⅓ cup black sesame seeds, toasted
- 1 tsp olive oil
- 1 can chickpeas
- ½ cup almonds, toasted
- 2 tbsp coriander seeds
- 1 tbsp cumin seeds, toasted
- 2 tsp fennel seeds, toasted
- Salt and black pepper to taste

Directions:

1. Preheat oven to 400 F. Spread the chickpeas in a single layer on a baking sheet and drizzle with olive oil. Roast for 40-45 minutes until browned and crisp, stirring every 5-10 minutes. Remove and let cool completely.

2. Blend the remaining ingredients in your food processor and remove to a bowl. Pour the cooled chickpeas into the food processor and pulse until coarsely ground. Mix them with the almonds and seeds until well combined. Store the spices in an airtight container at room temperature for up to 1 month.

Nutrition Info:

- Info Per Serving: Calories: 198;Fat: 3.0g;Protein: 2.1g;Carbs: 5g.

Eggplant & Sweet Potato Salad

Servings:4

Cooking Time:25 Minutes

Ingredients:

- 1 tbsp olive oil
- 4 cups arugula
- 2 baby eggplants, cubed
- 2 sweet potatoes, cubed
- 1 red onion, cut into wedges
- 1 tsp hot paprika
- 2 tsp cumin, ground
- Salt and black pepper to taste
- ¼ cup lime juice

Directions:

1. Warm the olive oil in a skillet over medium heat and cook eggplants and potatoes for 5 minutes. Stir in onion, paprika, cumin, salt, pepper, and lime juice and cook for another 10 minutes. Mix in arugula and serve.

Nutrition Info:

- Info Per Serving: Calories: 210;Fat: 9g;Protein: 5g;Carbs: 13g.

Chicken And Pastina Soup

Servings:6

Cooking Time: 20 Minutes

Ingredients:

- 1 tablespoon extra-virgin olive oil
- 2 garlic cloves, minced
- 3 cups packed chopped kale, center ribs removed
- 1 cup minced carrots
- 8 cups no-salt-added chicken or vegetable broth
- ¼ teaspoon kosher or sea salt
- ¼ teaspoon freshly ground black pepper
- ¾ cup uncooked acini de pepe or pastina pasta
- 2 cups shredded cooked chicken
- 3 tablespoons grated Parmesan cheese

Directions:

1. In a large stockpot over medium heat, heat the oil. Add the garlic and cook for 30 seconds, stirring frequently. Add the kale and carrots and cook for 5 minutes, stirring occasionally.

2. Add the broth, salt, and pepper, and turn the heat to high. Bring the broth to a boil, and add the pasta. Reduce the heat to medium and cook for 10 minutes, or until the pasta is cooked through, stirring every few minutes so the pasta doesn't stick to the bottom. Add the chicken, and cook for another 2 minutes to warm through.

3. Ladle the soup into six bowls. Top each with ½ tablespoon of cheese and serve.

Nutrition Info:

- Info Per Serving: Calories: 275;Fat: 19.0g;Protein: 16.0g;Carbs: 11.0g.

Beef Stew With Green Peas

Servings:4

Cooking Time:40 Minutes

Ingredients:

- 1 lb beef, tender cuts, boneless, cut into bits
- 2 tbsp olive oil
- 2 cups green peas
- 1 onion, diced
- 2 garlic cloves, minced
- 1 tomato, diced
- 3 cups beef broth
- ½ cup tomato paste
- 1 tsp cayenne pepper
- 1 tbsp flour
- Salt to taste
- ½ tsp dried thyme
- ½ tsp red pepper flakes

Directions:

1. Preheat your Instant Pot on Sauté mode and add warm the olive oil. Sear the meat for 6-8 minutes, stirring often. Add the onion, garlic, and salt and sauté for 3 more minutes. Stir in flour, thyme, and cayenne pepper for 1-2 minutes. Add in the tomato and tomato paste, stir, and pour in the stock.

2. Seal the lid, press Manual/Pressure Cook and cook for 20 minutes on High Pressure. When done, release the steam naturally for 10 minutes. Stir in the green peas, press Sauté, and cook for 4-5 minutes. Sprinkle with red pepper flakes.

Nutrition Info:

- Info Per Serving: Calories: 557;Fat: 16g;Protein: 78g;Carbs: 22g.

Basil Zucchini Marinara

Servings:4
Cooking Time:25 Minutes
Ingredients:

- 2 tbsp olive oil
- 1 shallot, chopped
- 1 garlic clove, minced
- 1 zucchini, sliced into rounds
- Salt and black pepper to taste
- 1 cup marinara sauce
- ¼ cup mozzarella, shredded
- 2 tbsp fresh basil, chopped

Directions:

1. Warm the olive oil in a skillet over medium heat. Sauté the shallot and garlic for 3 minutes until just tender and fragrant. Add in the zucchini and season with salt and pepper; cook for 4 minutes until lightly browned. Add marinara sauce and bring to a simmer; cook until zucchini is tender, 5-8 minutes. Scatter the mozzarella cheese on top of the zucchini layer and cover; heat for about 3 minutes until the cheese is melted. Sprinkle with basil and serve immediately.

Nutrition Info:

- Info Per Serving: Calories: 93;Fat: 7g;Protein: 3g;Carbs: 5g.

Barley, Parsley, And Pea Salad

Servings:4
Cooking Time: 10 Minutes
Ingredients:

- 2 cups water
- 1 cup quick-cooking barley
- 1 small bunch flat-leaf parsley, chopped
- 2 cups sugar snap pea pods
- Juice of 1 lemon
- ½ small red onion, diced
- 2 tablespoons extra-virgin olive oil
- Sea salt and freshly ground pepper, to taste

Directions:

1. Pour the water in a saucepan. Bring to a boil. Add the barley to the saucepan, then put the lid on.
2. Reduce the heat to low. Simmer the barley for 10 minutes or until the liquid is absorbed, then let sit for 5 minutes.
3. Open the lid, then transfer the barley in a colander and rinse under cold running water.
4. Pour the barley in a large salad bowl and add the remaining ingredients. Toss to combine well.
5. Serve immediately.

Nutrition Info:

- Info Per Serving: Calories: 152;Fat: 7.4g;Protein: 3.7g;Carbs: 19.3g.

Favorite Green Bean Stir-fry

Servings:4
Cooking Time:15 Minutes
Ingredients:

- 1 tbsp olive oil
- 1 tbsp butter
- 1 fennel bulb, sliced
- 1 red onion, sliced
- 4 cloves garlic, pressed
- 1 lb green beans, steamed
- ½ tsp dried oregano
- 2 tbsp balsamic vinegar
- Salt and black pepper to taste

Directions:

1. Heat the butter and olive oil a saucepan over medium heat. Add in the onion and garlic and sauté for 3 minutes. Stir in oregano, fennel, balsamic vinegar, salt, and pepper. Stir-fry for another 6-8 minutes and add in the green beans; cook for 2-3 minutes. Adjust the seasoning and serve.

Nutrition Info:

- Info Per Serving: Calories: 126;Fat: 6g;Protein: 3.3g;Carbs: 16.6g.

Chicken & Stelline Pasta Soup

Servings:4
Cooking Time:40 Minutes
Ingredients:

- 2 tbsp olive oil
- 1 onion, chopped
- 2 garlic cloves, minced
- 1 celery stalk, chopped
- 1 carrot, chopped
- 4 cups chicken stock
- Salt and black pepper to taste
- ¼ cup lemon juice
- 1 chicken breast, cubed
- ½ cup stelline pasta
- 6 mint leaves, chopped

Directions:

1. Warm the olive oil in a pot over medium heat and sauté onion, garlic, celery, and carrot for 5 minutes until tender. Add in the chicken and cook for another 4-5 minutes, stirring occasionally. Pour in chicken stock and bring to a boil; cook for 10 minutes. Add in the stelline pasta and let simmer for 10 minutes. Stir in lemon juice and adjust the seasoning with salt and pepper. Sprinkle with mint and serve immediately.

Nutrition Info:

- Info Per Serving: Calories: 240;Fat: 12g;Protein: 13g;Carbs: 15g.

Easy Romesco Sauce

Servings:6
Cooking Time:10 Minutes
Ingredients:

- 1 jar roasted red peppers, drained
- 1 can diced tomatoes, undrained
- 2 garlic cloves, crushed
- 2 tsp sherry vinegar
- ½ cup dry-roasted almonds
- ⅔ cup day-old bread, torn
- 1 tsp smoked paprika
- ¼ cup extra-virgin olive oil
- Salt and black pepper to taste
- 1 tsp crushed red chili flakes

Directions:

1. Place the roasted peppers, tomatoes and their juices, almonds, garlic, vinegar, smoked paprika, salt, and pepper in your food processor. Blitz the ingredients on medium speed and slowly drizzle in the olive oil with the blender running until the dip is thoroughly mixed. Add the bread and red chili flakes and blend. Serve and enjoy!

Nutrition Info:

- Info Per Serving: Calories: 96;Fat: 6.8g;Protein: 3.2g;Carbs: 8.1g.

Yogurt Cucumber Salad

Servings:4
Cooking Time:10 Min + Chilling Time
Ingredients:

- 1 tbsp olive oil
- 2 tbsp walnuts, ground
- 1 cup Greek yogurt
- 2 garlic cloves, minced
- Salt and white pepper to taste
- 1 tbsp wine vinegar
- 1 tbsp dill, chopped
- 3 medium cucumbers, sliced
- 1 tbsp chives, chopped

Directions:

1. Combine cucumbers, walnuts, garlic, salt, pepper, vinegar, yogurt, dill, olive oil, and chives in a bowl. Let sit in the fridge for 1 hour. Serve.

Nutrition Info:

- Info Per Serving: Calories: 220;Fat: 13g;Protein: 4g;Carbs: 9g.

Garlic Herb Butter

Servings:4
Cooking Time:5 Minutes
Ingredients:

- ½ cup butter, softened
- 1 garlic clove, finely minced
- 2 tsp fresh rosemary, chopped
- 1 tsp marjoram, chopped
- Salt to taste

Directions:

1. Blend the butter, garlic, rosemary, marjoram, and salt in your food processor until the mixture is well combined, smooth, and creamy, scraping down the sides as necessary. Scrape the butter mixture with a spatula into a glass container and cover. Store in the refrigerator for up to 30 days.

Nutrition Info:

- Info Per Serving: Calories: 103;Fat: 12.4g;Protein: 0g;Carbs: 0g.

Roasted Root Vegetable Soup

Servings:6
Cooking Time: 35 Minutes
Ingredients:

- 2 parsnips, peeled and sliced
- 2 carrots, peeled and sliced
- 2 sweet potatoes, peeled and sliced
- 1 teaspoon chopped fresh rosemary
- 1 teaspoon chopped fresh thyme
- 1 teaspoon sea salt
- ½ teaspoon freshly ground black pepper
- 2 tablespoons extra-virgin olive oil
- 4 cups low-sodium vegetable soup
- ½ cup grated Parmesan cheese, for garnish (optional)

Directions:

1. Preheat the oven to 400ºF. Line a baking sheet with aluminum foil.
2. Combine the parsnips, carrots, and sweet potatoes in a large bowl, then sprinkle with rosemary, thyme, salt, and pepper, and drizzle with olive oil. Toss to coat the vegetables well.
3. Arrange the vegetables on the baking sheet, then roast in the preheated oven for 30 minutes or until lightly browned and soft. Flip the vegetables halfway through the roasting.
4. Pour the roasted vegetables with vegetable broth in a food processor, then pulse until creamy and smooth.
5. Pour the puréed vegetables in a saucepan, then warm over low heat until heated through.
6. Spoon the soup in a large serving bowl, then scatter with Parmesan cheese. Serve immediately.

Nutrition Info:

- Info Per Serving: Calories: 192;Fat: 5.7g;Protein: 4.8g;Carbs: 31.5g.

Fancy Turkish Salad

Servings:6
Cooking Time:15 Minutes

Ingredients:

- 2 pieces of pita bread, broken into pieces
- 3 tbsp olive oil
- 2 tbsp butter
- 3 medium tomatoes, chopped
- 1 cucumber, sliced
- 1 cup baby spinach
- 5 green bell peppers, chopped
- 5 radishes, sliced
- 1 lime, juiced
- Salt and black pepper to taste
- ½ tsp cinnamon powder
- ¼ tsp allspice, ground

Directions:

1. Warm the butter in a skillet over medium heat and cook pita for 5 minutes. Remove and season with salt and pepper.
2. Combine cooked pita, cucumber, spinach, tomatoes, bell pepper, and radishes in a bowl. Mix olive oil, lime juice, salt, pepper, cinnamon powder, and allspice in another bowl and pour over the salad. Toss to coat. Serve immediately.

Nutrition Info:

- Info Per Serving: Calories: 280;Fat: 8g;Protein: 12g;Carbs: 27g.

Classic Zuppa Toscana

Servings:4
Cooking Time:25 Minutes

Ingredients:

- 2 tbsp olive oil
- 1 yellow onion, chopped
- 4 garlic cloves, minced
- 1 celery stalk, chopped
- 1 carrot, chopped
- 15 oz canned tomatoes, diced
- 1 zucchini, chopped
- 6 cups vegetable stock
- 2 tbsp tomato paste
- 15 oz canned white beans
- 5 oz Tuscan kale
- 1 tbsp basil, chopped
- Salt and black pepper to taste

Directions:

1. Warm the olive oil in a pot over medium heat. Cook garlic and onion for 3 minutes. Stir in celery, carrot, tomatoes, zucchini, stock, tomato paste, white beans, kale, salt, and pepper and bring to a simmer. Cook for 10 minutes. Top with basil.

Nutrition Info:

- Info Per Serving: Calories: 480;Fat: 9g;Protein: 28g;Carbs: 77g.

Mushroom-barley Soup

Servings:6

Cooking Time:10 Minutes

Ingredients:

- 3 tbsp olive oil
- 1 onion, chopped
- 1 cup carrots, chopped
- ½ cup celery, chopped
- 1 cup mushrooms, chopped
- 6 cups vegetable broth
- 1 cup pearl barley
- 2 tbsp tomato paste
- ½ tsp dried thyme
- ½ cup Parmesan cheese

Directions:

1. Warm the olive oil in a large stockpot over medium heat. Add the onion, celery, and carrots and cook for 5 minutes, stirring frequently. Add the mushrooms and cook for 3 minutes until tender. Pour in the broth, barley, tomato paste, and thyme. Bring the soup to a boil. Simmer for another 15-18 minutes until the barley is cooked through. Top with cheese and serve.

Nutrition Info:

- Info Per Serving: Calories: 195;Fat: 4.2g;Protein: 7g;Carbs: 33.8g.

Mushroom & Parmesan Risotto

Servings:4

Cooking Time:25 Minutes

Ingredients:

- 1 ½ cups mixed mushrooms, sliced
- 3 tbsp olive oil
- 1 shallot, chopped
- 1 cup Arborio rice
- 4 cups vegetable stock
- 2 tbsp dry white wine
- 1 cup grated Parmesan cheese
- 2 tbsp butter
- 2 tbsp fresh parsley, chopped

Directions:

1. Pour the vegetable stock into a small saucepan over low heat and bring to a simmer; then turn the heat off.

2. Warm the olive oil in a large saucepan over medium heat. Sauté the mushrooms and shallot for 6 minutes until tender. Stir in rice for 3 minutes until opaque. Pour in the wine and stir. Gradually add the hot stock to the rice mixture, about 1 ladleful at a time, stirring until the liquid is absorbed. Remove the saucepan from the heat, stir in butter and 3 tbsp of Parmesan cheese. Cover and leave to rest for 5 minutes. Scatter the remaining cheese and parsley over the risotto and serve in bowls.

Nutrition Info:

- Info Per Serving: Calories: 354;Fat: 29g;Protein: 11g;Carbs: 22g.

Warm Kale Salad With Red Bell Pepper

Servings:4

Cooking Time:15 Minutes

Ingredients:

- 1 tbsp olive oil
- 4 cups kale, torn
- 2 cloves garlic, minced
- 1 red bell pepper, diced
- Salt and black pepper to taste
- ½ lemon, juiced

Directions:

1. Warm the olive oil in a large skillet over medium heat and add the garlic. Cook for 1 minute, and then add the bell pepper. Cook for 4-5 minutes until the pepper is tender. Stir in the kale. Cook for 3-4 minutes or just until wilted, then remove from heat. Place pepper and kale in a bowl and season with salt and black pepper. Drizzle with lemon juice.

Nutrition Info:

- Info Per Serving: Calories: 123;Fat: 4g;Protein: 6g;Carbs: 22g.

Turkish Chickpeas

Servings:4

Cooking Time:40 Minutes

Ingredients:

- 3 tbsp olive oil
- 2 cans chickpeas
- 2 tsp smoked paprika
- ½ tsp ground coriander
- ½ tsp cumin
- ½ tsp dried oregano
- Salt and white pepper to taste

Directions:

1. Preheat the oven to 400 F. Spread the chickpeas onto a greased baking sheet. In a bowl, combine the olive oil, paprika, ground coriander, cumin, oregano, salt, and white pepper. Pour the mixture over the chickpeas and toss to combine. Bake for 30 minutes or until the chickpeas turn golden brown, shaking once or twice the baking sheet.

Nutrition Info:

- Info Per Serving: Calories: 308;Fat: 13g;Protein: 11g;Carbs: 40g.

Homemade Herbes De Provence Spice

Servings:4

Cooking Time:5 Minutes

Ingredients:

- 2 tbsp dried oregano
- 2 tbsp dried thyme
- 2 tbsp dried marjoram
- 2 tbsp dried rosemary
- 2 tsp fennel seeds, toasted

Directions:

1. Mix the oregano, thyme, marjoram, rosemary, and fennel seeds in a bowl. Store the spices in an airtight container at room temperature for up to 7-9 months.

Nutrition Info:

- Info Per Serving: Calories: 32;Fat: 1.1g;Protein: 1.4g;Carbs: 6.0g.

Bean & Zucchini Soup

Servings:4
Cooking Time:40 Minutes
Ingredients:

- 1 tbsp olive oil
- 1 onion, chopped
- 2 cloves garlic, minced
- 5 cups vegetable broth
- 1 cup dried chickpeas
- ½ cup pinto beans, soaked
- ½ cup navy beans, soaked
- 3 carrots, chopped
- 1 large celery stalk, chopped
- 1 tsp dried thyme
- 16 oz zucchini noodles
- Salt and black pepper to taste

Directions:

1. Warm the olive oil on Sauté in your Instant Pot. Stir in garlic and onion and cook for 5 minutes until golden brown. Mix in pepper, broth, carrots, salt, pepper, celery, beans, chickpeas, and thyme. Seal the lid and cook for 15 minutes on High Pressure. Release the pressure naturally for 10 minutes. Mix zucchini noodles into the soup and stir until wilted. Serve.

Nutrition Info:

- Info Per Serving: Calories: 481;Fat: 8g;Protein: 23g;Carbs: 83g.

Sun-dried Tomato & Spinach Pasta Salad

Servings:4
Cooking Time:45 Min + Cooling Time
Ingredients:

- 1 ½ cups farfalle
- 1 cup chopped baby spinach, rinsed and dried
- 8 sun-dried tomatoes, sliced
- 1 carrot, grated
- 2 scallions, thinly sliced
- 1 garlic clove, minced
- 1 dill pickle, diced
- ⅔ cup extra-virgin olive oil
- 1 tbsp red wine vinegar
- 1 tbsp lemon juice
- ½ cup Greek yogurt
- 1 tsp chopped fresh oregano
- Salt and black pepper to taste
- 1 cup feta cheese, crumbled

Directions:

1. Bring a large pot of salted water to a boil, add the farfalle, and cook for 7-9 minutes until al dente. Drain the pasta and set aside to cool. In a large bowl, combine spinach, sun-dried tomatoes, carrot, scallions, garlic, and pickle. Add pasta and toss to combine. In a medium bowl, whisk olive oil, vinegar, lemon juice, yogurt, oregano, pepper, and salt. Add dressing to pasta and toss to coat. Sprinkle with feta cheese and serve.

Nutrition Info:

- Info Per Serving: Calories: 239;Fat: 14g;Protein: 8g;Carbs: 20g.

Restaurant-style Zuppa Di Fagioli

Servings:4

Cooking Time:10 Minutes

Ingredients:

- 2 tbsp Pecorino cheese, grated
- 2 tbsp olive oil
- 1 carrot, peeled and diced
- 1 onion, chopped
- 2 cloves garlic, chopped
- 4 cups chicken broth
- ½ cup white beans, soaked
- 1 tsp dried thyme
- Salt and black pepper to taste
- 4 whole-wheat bread slices

Directions:

1. Warm the olive oil in a large stockpot over medium heat. Add the carrot and onion and sauté until the onion is translucent. Stir-fry the garlic for 1 more minute. Pour in the broth, beans, salt, and pepper, and cover. Bring to a boil and simmer for 2 hours or until the beans are tender. Adjust the taste and top with Pecorino cheese. Serve with toasted whole-wheat bread.

Nutrition Info:

- Info Per Serving: Calories: 186;Fat: 3g;Protein: 6g;Carbs: 24g.

Gorgonzola, Fig & Prosciutto Salad

Servings:2

Cooking Time:15 Minutes

Ingredients:

- 2 tbsp crumbled Gorgonzola cheese
- 2 tbsp olive oil
- 3 cups Romaine lettuce, torn
- 4 figs, sliced
- 3 thin prosciutto slices
- ¼ cup pecan halves, toasted
- 1 tbsp balsamic vinegar

Directions:

1. Toss lettuce and figs in a large bowl. Drizzle with olive oil. Slice the prosciutto lengthwise into 1-inch strips. Add the prosciutto, pecans, and Gorgonzola cheese to the bowl. Toss the salad lightly. Drizzle with balsamic vinegar.

Nutrition Info:

- Info Per Serving: Calories: 519;Fat: 38g;Protein: 20g;Carbs: 29g.

Artichoke And Arugula Salad

Servings:6

Cooking Time: 0 Minutes

Ingredients:

- Salad:
- 6 canned oil-packed artichoke hearts, sliced
- 6 cups baby arugula leaves
- 6 fresh olives, pitted and chopped
- 1 cup cherry tomatoes, sliced in half
- Dressing:
- 1 teaspoon Dijon mustard
- 2 tablespoons balsamic vinegar
- 1 clove garlic, minced
- 2 tablespoons extra-virgin olive oil
- For Garnish:
- 4 fresh basil leaves, thinly sliced

Directions:

1. Combine the ingredients for the salad in a large salad bowl, then toss to combine well.
2. Combine the ingredients for the dressing in a small bowl, then stir to mix well.
3. Dressing the salad, then serve with basil leaves on top.

Nutrition Info:

- Info Per Serving: Calories: 134;Fat: 12.1g;Protein: 1.6g;Carbs: 6.2g.

Beans , Grains, And Pastas Recipes

Hot Collard Green Oats With Parmesan

Servings:4
Cooking Time:15 Minutes
Ingredients:

- 2 tbsp olive oil
- 2 cups collard greens, torn
- ½ cup black olives, sliced
- 1 cup rolled oats
- 2 tomatoes, diced
- 2 spring onions, chopped
- 1 tsp garlic powder
- ½ tsp hot paprika
- A pinch of salt
- 2 tbsp fresh parsley, chopped
- 1 tbsp lemon juice
- ½ cup Parmesan cheese, grated

Directions:

1. Put 2 cups of water in a pot over medium heat. Bring to a boil, then lower the heat, and add the rolled oats. Cook for 4-5 minutes. Mix in tomatoes, spring onions, hot paprika, garlic powder, salt, collard greens, black olives, parsley, lemon juice, and olive oil. Cook for another 5 minutes. Ladle into bowls and top with Parmesan cheese. Serve warm.

Nutrition Info:

- Info Per Serving: Calories: 192;Fat: 11g;Protein: 5g;Carbs: 19.8g.

Veggie & Beef Ragu

Servings:4
Cooking Time:20 Minutes
Ingredients:

- 2 tbsp butter
- 16 oz tagliatelle pasta
- 1 lb ground beef
- Salt and black pepper to taste
- ¼ cup tomato sauce
- 1 green bell pepper, chopped
- 1 red bell pepper, chopped
- 1 small red onion, chopped
- 1 cup grated Parmesan cheese

Directions:

1. In a pot of boiling water, cook the tagliatelle pasta for 8-10 minutes until al dente. Drain and set aside.
2. Heat half of the butter in a medium skillet and cook the beef until brown, 5 minutes. Season with salt and black pepper. Stir in the tomato sauce and cook for 10 minutes or until the sauce reduces by a quarter. Stir in the bell peppers and onion; cook for 1 minute and turn the heat off. Adjust the taste with salt and black pepper and mix in the tagliatelle. Dish the food onto serving plates. Garnish with Parmesan.

Nutrition Info:

- Info Per Serving: Calories: 451;Fat: 26g;Protein: 39g;Carbs: 6g.

Arrabbiata Penne Rigate

Servings:4
Cooking Time:30 Minutes
Ingredients:

- 2 tbsp olive oil
- 1 onion, chopped
- 6 cloves garlic, minced
- ½ red chili, chopped
- 2 cups canned tomatoes, diced
- ½ tsp sugar
- Salt and black pepper to taste
- 1 lb penne rigate
- 1 cup shredded mozzarella
- 1 cup fresh basil, chopped
- ½ cup grated Parmesan cheese

Directions:

1. Bring a large pot of salted water to a boil, add the penne, and cook for 7-9 minutes until al dente. Reserve ¼ cup pasta cooking water and drain pasta. Set aside.
2. Warm the oil in a saucepan over medium heat. Sauté the onion and garlic for 3-5 minutes or until softened. Add tomatoes with their liquid, black pepper, sugar, and salt. Cook 20 minutes or until the sauce thickens. Add the pasta and reserved cooking water and stir for 2-3 minutes. Add mozzarella cheese and red chili and cook until the cheese melts, 3-4 minutes. Top with Parmesan and basil and serve.

Nutrition Info:

- Info Per Serving: Calories: 454;Fat: 12g;Protein: 18g;Carbs: 70g.

Mediterranean-style Beans And Greens

Servings:2
Cooking Time: 15 Minutes
Ingredients:

- 1 can diced tomatoes with juice
- 1 can cannellini beans, drained and rinsed
- 2 tablespoons chopped green olives, plus 1 or 2 sliced for garnish
- ¼ cup vegetable broth, plus more as needed
- 1 teaspoon extra-virgin olive oil
- 2 cloves garlic, minced
- 4 cups arugula
- ¼ cup freshly squeezed lemon juice

Directions:

1. In a medium saucepan, bring the tomatoes, beans and chopped olives to a low boil, adding just enough broth to make the ingredients saucy (you may need more than ¼ cup if your canned tomatoes don't have a lot of juice). Reduce heat to low and simmer for about 5 minutes.
2. Meanwhile, in a large skillet, heat the olive oil over medium-high heat. When the oil is hot and starts to shimmer, add garlic and sauté just until it starts to turn slightly tan, about 30 seconds. Add the arugula and lemon juice, stirring to coat leaves with the olive oil and juice. Cover and reduce heat to low. Simmer for 3 to 5 minutes.
3. Serve beans over the greens and garnish with olive slices.

Nutrition Info:

- Info Per Serving: Calories: 262;Fat: 5.9g;Protein: 13.2g;Carbs: 40.4g.

Tasty Beanballs In Marinara Sauce

Servings:4
Cooking Time:45 Minutes
Ingredients:

- Beanballs
- 2 tbsp olive oil
- ½ yellow onion, minced
- 1 tsp coriander seeds
- ½ tsp dried oregano
- ½ tsp dried thyme
- ½ tsp red pepper flakes
- 1 tsp garlic powder
- 1 can white beans
- ½ cup bread crumbs
- Salt and black pepper to taste
- Marinara
- 1 can diced tomatoes with juice
- 1 tbsp olive oil
- 3 garlic cloves, minced
- 2 tbsp basil leaves
- Salt to taste

Directions:

1. Preheat the oven to 350 F. Warm 2 tbsp of olive oil in a skillet over medium heat. Sauté the onion for 3 minutes. Sprinkle with coriander seeds, oregano, thyme, pepper flakes, and garlic powder, then cook for 1 minute or until aromatic.

2. Pour the sautéed mixture into a food processor and add the beans and bread crumbs. Sprinkle with salt and black pepper and pulse to combine well, and the mixture holds together. Shape the mixture into balls. Arrange them on a greased baking sheet. Bake for 30 minutes or until lightly browned. Flip the balls halfway through the cooking time.

3. Meanwhile, heat 1 tbsp of olive oil in a saucepan over medium heat. Add the garlic and basil and sauté for 2 minutes or until fragrant. Fold in the tomatoes and juice. Bring to a boil. Reduce the heat to low. Put the lid on and simmer for 15 minutes. Sprinkle with salt. Transfer the beanballs to a large plate and drizzle with marinara sauce. Serve.

Nutrition Info:

- Info Per Serving: Calories: 351;Fat: 16g;Protein: 12g;Carbs: 43g.

Valencian-style Mussel Rice

Servings:4
Cooking Time:40 Minutes
Ingredients:

- 1 lb mussels, cleaned and debearded
- 2 tbsp olive oil
- 2 garlic cloves, minced
- 1 yellow onion, chopped
- 2 tomatoes, chopped
- 2 cups fish stock
- 1 cup white rice
- 1 bunch parsley, chopped
- Salt and white pepper to taste

Directions:

1. Warm the olive oil in a pot over medium heat and cook onion and garlic for 5 minutes. Stir in rice for 1 minute. Pour in tomatoes and fish stock and bring to a boil. Add in the mussels and simmer for 20 minutes. Discard any unopened mussels. Adjust the taste with salt and white pepper. Serve topped with parsley.

Nutrition Info:

- Info Per Serving: Calories: 310;Fat: 15g;Protein: 12g;Carbs: 17g.

Spinach & Salmon Fettuccine In White Sauce

Servings:4

Cooking Time:35 Minutes

Ingredients:

- 5 tbsp butter
- 16 oz fettuccine
- 4 salmon fillets, cubed
- Salt and black pepper to taste
- 3 garlic cloves, minced
- 1 ¼ cups heavy cream
- ½ cup dry white wine
- 1 tsp grated lemon zest
- 1 cup baby spinach
- Lemon wedges for garnishing

Directions:

1. In a pot of boiling water, cook the fettuccine pasta for 8-10 minutes until al dente. Drain and set aside.

2. Melt half of the butter in a large skillet; season the salmon with salt, black pepper, and cook in the butter until golden brown on all sides and flaky within, 8 minutes. Transfer to a plate and set aside.

3. Add the remaining butter to the skillet to melt and stir in the garlic. Cook until fragrant, 1 minute. Mix in heavy cream, white wine, lemon zest, salt, and pepper. Allow boiling over low heat for 5 minutes. Stir in spinach, allow wilting for 2 minutes and stir in fettuccine and salmon until well-coated in the sauce. Garnish with lemon wedges.

Nutrition Info:

- Info Per Serving: Calories: 795;Fat: 46g;Protein: 72g;Carbs: 20g.

Wild Rice With Cheese & Mushrooms

Servings:4

Cooking Time:30 Minutes

Ingredients:

- 2 cups chicken stock
- 1 cup wild rice
- 1 onion, chopped
- ½ lb wild mushrooms, sliced
- 2 garlic cloves, minced
- 1 lemon, juiced and zested
- 1 tbsp chives, chopped
- ½ cup mozzarella, grated
- Salt and black pepper to taste

Directions:

1. Warm chicken stock in a pot over medium heat and add in wild rice, onion, mushrooms, garlic, lemon juice, lemon zest, salt, and pepper. Bring to a simmer and cook for 20 minutes. Transfer to a baking tray and top with mozzarella cheese. Place the tray under the broiler for 4 minutes until the cheese is melted. Sprinkle with chives and serve.

Nutrition Info:

- Info Per Serving: Calories: 230;Fat: 6g;Protein: 6g;Carbs: 13g.

Italian Tarragon Buckwheat

Servings:6
Cooking Time:55 Minutes

Ingredients:

- 3 tbsp olive oil
- 1 ½ cups buckwheat, soaked
- 3 cups vegetable broth
- ½ onion, finely chopped
- 1 garlic clove, minced
- 2 tsp fresh tarragon, minced
- Salt and black pepper to taste
- 2 oz Parmesan cheese, grated
- 2 tbsp parsley, minced
- 2 tsp lemon juice

Directions:

1. Pulse buckwheat in your blender until about half of the grains are broken into smaller pieces. Bring broth and 3 cups of water to a boil in a medium saucepan over high heat. Reduce heat to low, cover, and keep warm.

2. Warm 2 tablespoons oil in a pot over medium heat. Add onion and cook until softened, 5 minutes. Stir in garlic and cook until fragrant, about 30 seconds. Add farro and cook, stirring frequently, until grains are lightly toasted, 3 minutes.

3. Stir 5 cups warm broth mixture into farro mixture, reduce heat to low, cover, and cook until almost all liquid has been absorbed and farro is just al dente, about 25 minutes, stirring twice during cooking.

4. Add tarragon, salt, and pepper and keep stirring for 5 minutes. Remove from heat and stir in Parmesan cheese, parsley, lemon juice, and the remaining olive oil. Adjust the seasoning and serve.

Nutrition Info:

- Info Per Serving: Calories: 321;Fat: 21g;Protein: 15g;Carbs: 35g.

Lebanese Flavor Broken Thin Noodles

Servings:6
Cooking Time: 25 Minutes

Ingredients:

- 1 tablespoon extra-virgin olive oil
- 1 cup vermicelli, broken into 1- to 1½-inch pieces
- 3 cups shredded cabbage
- 1 cup brown rice
- 3 cups low-sodium vegetable soup
- ½ cup water
- 2 garlic cloves, mashed
- ¼ teaspoon sea salt
- ⅛ teaspoon crushed red pepper flakes
- ½ cup coarsely chopped cilantro
- Fresh lemon slices, for serving

Directions:

1. Heat the olive oil in a saucepan over medium-high heat until shimmering.
2. Add the vermicelli and sauté for 3 minutes or until toasted.
3. Add the cabbage and sauté for 4 minutes or until tender.
4. Pour in the brown rice, vegetable soup, and water. Add the garlic and sprinkle with salt and red pepper flakes.
5. Bring to a boil over high heat. Reduce the heat to medium low. Put the lid on and simmer for another 10 minutes.
6. Turn off the heat, then let sit for 5 minutes without opening the lid.
7. Pour them on a large serving platter and spread with cilantro. Squeeze the lemon slices over and serve warm.

Nutrition Info:

- Info Per Serving: Calories: 127;Fat: 3.1g;Protein: 4.2g;Carbs: 22.9g.

Easy Simple Pesto Pasta

Servings:4
Cooking Time: 8 Minutes

Ingredients:

- 1 pound spaghetti
- 4 cups fresh basil leaves, stems removed
- 3 cloves garlic
- 1 teaspoon salt
- ½ teaspoon freshly ground black pepper
- ½ cup toasted pine nuts
- ¼ cup lemon juice
- ½ cup grated Parmesan cheese
- 1 cup extra-virgin olive oil

Directions:

1. Bring a large pot of salted water to a boil. Add the spaghetti to the pot and cook for 8 minutes.
2. In a food processor, place the remaining ingredients, except for the olive oil, and pulse.
3. While the processor is running, slowly drizzle the olive oil through the top opening. Process until all the olive oil has been added.
4. Reserve ½ cup of the cooking liquid. Drain the pasta and put it into a large bowl. Add the pesto and cooking liquid to the bowl of pasta and toss everything together.
5. Serve immediately.

Nutrition Info:

- Info Per Serving: Calories: 1067;Fat: 72.0g;Protein: 23.0g;Carbs: 91g.

Creamy Saffron Chicken With Ziti

Servings:4
Cooking Time:35 Minutes

Ingredients:

- 3 tbsp butter
- 16 oz ziti
- 4 chicken breasts, cut into strips
- ½ tsp ground saffron threads
- 1 yellow onion, chopped
- 2 garlic cloves, minced
- 1 tbsp almond flour
- 1 pinch cardamom powder
- 1 pinch cinnamon powder
- 1 cup heavy cream
- 1 cup chicken stock
- ¼ cup chopped scallions
- 3 tbsp chopped parsley
- Salt and black pepper to taste

Directions:

1. In a pot of boiling water, cook the ziti pasta for 8-10 minutes until al dente. Drain and set aside.
2. Melt the butter in a large skillet, season the chicken with salt, black pepper, and cook in the oil until golden brown on the outside, 5 minutes. Stir in the saffron, onion, garlic and cook until the onion softens and the garlic and saffron are fragrant, 3 minutes. Stir in the almond flour, cardamom powder, and cinnamon powder, and cook for 1 minute to exude some fragrance. Add the heavy cream, chicken stock and cook for 2 to 3 minutes. Adjust the taste with salt, pepper and mix in the ziti and scallions. Allow warming for 1-2 minutes and turn the heat off. Garnish with parsley.

Nutrition Info:

- Info Per Serving: Calories: 775;Fat: 48g;Protein: 73g;Carbs: 3g.

Ribollita (tuscan Bean Soup)

Servings:6
Cooking Time:1 Hour 45 Minutes
Ingredients:

- 3 tbsp olive oil
- Salt and black pepper to taste
- 2 cups canned cannellini beans
- 6 oz pancetta, chopped
- ¼ tsp red pepper flakes
- 1 onion, chopped
- 2 carrots, chopped
- 1 celery rib, chopped
- 3 garlic cloves, minced
- 4 cups chicken broth
- 1 lb lacinato kale, chopped
- 1 can diced tomatoes
- 1 rosemary sprig, chopped
- Crusty bread for serving

Directions:

1. Warm the olive oil in a skillet over medium heat and add the pancetta. Cook, stirring occasionally, until pancetta is lightly browned and fat has rendered, 5-6 minutes. Add onion, carrots, and celery and cook, stirring occasionally, until softened and lightly browned, 4-6 minutes. Stir in garlic and red pepper flakes and cook until fragrant, 1 minute.

2. Stir in broth, 2 cups of water, and beans and bring to a boil. Cover and simmer for 15 minutes. Stir in lacinato kale and tomatoes and cook for another 5 minutes. Sprinkle with rosemary and adjust the taste. Serve with crusty bread.

Nutrition Info:

- Info Per Serving: Calories: 385;Fat: 18g;Protein: 36g;Carbs: 25g.

Garlic And Parsley Chickpeas

Servings:4
Cooking Time: 18 To 20 Minutes
Ingredients:

- ¼ cup extra-virgin olive oil, divided
- 4 garlic cloves, sliced thinly
- ⅛ teaspoon red pepper flakes
- 1 onion, chopped finely
- ¼ teaspoon salt, plus more to taste
- Black pepper, to taste
- 2 cans chickpeas, rinsed
- 1 cup vegetable broth
- 2 tablespoons minced fresh parsley
- 2 teaspoons lemon juice

Directions:

1. Add 3 tablespoons of the olive oil, garlic, and pepper flakes to a skillet over medium heat. Cook for about 3 minutes, stirring constantly, or until the garlic turns golden but not brown.

2. Stir in the onion and ¼ teaspoon salt and cook for 5 to 7 minutes, or until softened and lightly browned.

3. Add the chickpeas and broth to the skillet and bring to a simmer. Reduce the heat to medium-low, cover, and cook for about 7 minutes, or until the chickpeas are cooked through and flavors meld.

4. Uncover, increase the heat to high and continue to cook for about 3 minutes more, or until nearly all liquid has evaporated.

5. Turn off the heat, stir in the parsley and lemon juice. Season to taste with salt and pepper and drizzle with remaining 1 tablespoon of the olive oil.

6. Serve warm.

Nutrition Info:

- Info Per Serving: Calories: 220;Fat: 11.4g;Protein: 6.5g;Carbs: 24.6g.

Caprese Pasta With Roasted Asparagus

Servings:6

Cooking Time: 25 Minutes

Ingredients:

- 8 ounces uncooked small pasta, like orecchiette (little ears) or farfalle (bow ties)
- 1½ pounds fresh asparagus, ends trimmed and stalks chopped into 1-inch pieces
- 1½ cups grape tomatoes, halved
- 2 tablespoons extra-virgin olive oil
- ¼ teaspoon kosher salt
- ¼ teaspoon freshly ground black pepper
- 2 cups fresh Mozzarella, drained and cut into bite-size pieces
- ⅓ cup torn fresh basil leaves
- 2 tablespoons balsamic vinegar

Directions:

1. Preheat the oven to 400ºF.

2. In a large stockpot of salted water, cook the pasta for about 8 to 10 minutes. Drain and reserve about ¼ cup of the cooking liquid.

3. Meanwhile, in a large bowl, toss together the asparagus, tomatoes, oil, salt and pepper. Spread the mixture onto a large, rimmed baking sheet and bake in the oven for 15 minutes, stirring twice during cooking.

4. Remove the vegetables from the oven and add the cooked pasta to the baking sheet. Mix with a few tablespoons of cooking liquid to help the sauce become smoother and the saucy vegetables stick to the pasta.

5. Gently mix in the Mozzarella and basil. Drizzle with the balsamic vinegar. Serve from the baking sheet or pour the pasta into a large bowl.

Nutrition Info:

- Info Per Serving: Calories: 147;Fat: 3.0g;Protein: 16.0g;Carbs: 17.0g.

One-bowl Microwave Lasagna

Servings:2

Cooking Time:30 Minutes

Ingredients:

- ½ tbsp chopped basil
- ½ lb ground beef, crumbled
- 1 cup tomatoes, diced
- 1 ½ cups marinara sauce
- 1 ½ cups mozzarella, grated
- 1 ½ cups ricotta cheese
- 12 oven-ready lasagna noodles

Directions:

1. Microwave the crumbled beef in a microwave-safe bowl for 5 minutes. Stir and microwave for 4 more minutes until the beef is cooked through. Remove and mix the ground beef with tomatoes and marinara sauce. Stir in cheeses.

2. Place 4 lasagna noodles in a large bowl. Spread 1/3 of the meat mixture over the noodle layer. Repeat until you run out of ingredients. Cover the bowl with parchment paper. Microwave for about 8 minutes until cheeses are cooked. Let lasagna stand for 10 minutes. Top with basil. Serve.

Nutrition Info:

- Info Per Serving: Calories: 917;Fat: 34g;Protein: 85g;Carbs: 73g.

Spinach Farfalle With Ricotta Cheese

Servings:4

Cooking Time:25 Minutes

Ingredients:

- ¼ cup extra-virgin olive oil
- ½ cup crumbled ricotta cheese
- 2 tbsp black olives, halved
- 4 cups fresh baby spinach, chopped
- 2 tbsp scallions, chopped
- 16 oz farfalle pasta
- ¼ cup red wine vinegar
- 2 tsp lemon juice
- Salt and black pepper to taste

Directions:

1. Cook the farfalle pasta to pack instructions, drain and let it to cool. Mix the scallions, spinach, and cooled pasta in a bowl. Top with ricotta and olives. Combine the vinegar, olive oil, lemon juice, salt, and pepper in another bowl. Pour over the pasta mixture and toss to combine. Serve chilled.

Nutrition Info:

- Info Per Serving: Calories: 377;Fat: 16g;Protein: 12g;Carbs: 44g.

Cumin Rice Stuffed Bell Peppers

Servings:4

Cooking Time:35 Minutes

Ingredients:

- 1 tbsp olive oil
- 2 lb mixed bell peppers, halved
- 1 cup white rice, rinsed
- ½ cup ricotta cheese, crumbled
- 2 tomatoes, pureed
- 1 onion, chopped
- 1 tsp ground cumin
- 1 tsp ground fennel seeds
- Salt and black pepper to taste

Directions:

1. Blanch the peppers in a pot with salted water over medium heat for 1-2 minutes, drain and set aside. Add the rice to the pot, bring to a boil and simmer for 15 minutes. Drain and remove to a bowl. Add in olive oil, cumin, ground fennel seeds, onion, tomatoes, salt, and pepper and stir to combine. Divide the mixture between the pepper halves and top with ricotta cheese. Bake for 8-10 minutes. Serve right away.

Nutrition Info:

- Info Per Serving: Calories: 285;Fat: 6.7g;Protein: 8g;Carbs: 48.3g.

Jalapeño Veggie Rice Stew

Servings:4
Cooking Time:45 Minutes

Ingredients:

- 2 tbsp olive oil
- 1 cup rice
- 1 lb green beans, chopped
- 2 zucchinis, sliced
- 1 bell pepper, sliced
- 1 jalapeño pepper, chopped
- 1 carrot, chopped
- 2 spring onions, chopped
- 2 cloves garlic, minced
- 2 tomatoes, pureed
- 1 cup vegetable broth
- ½ tsp dried sage
- 1 tsp paprika
- Salt and black pepper to taste

Directions:

1. Cook the rice in a pot with 2 cups of water for about 20 minutes. Using a fork, fluff the rice and set aside. Heat the olive oil in a pot over medium heat. Add in the zucchinis, green beans, bell pepper, jalapeño pepper, carrot, spring onions, tomatoes, and garlic and stir-fry for 10 minutes or until the veggies are softened. Pour in vegetable broth, sage, paprika, salt, and black pepper. Cook covered for 7 minutes. Distribute the rice across bowls and top with the veggie mixture. Serve hot.

Nutrition Info:

- Info Per Serving: Calories: 153;Fat: 7.9g;Protein: 5.7g;Carbs: 19g.

Greek-style Shrimp & Feta Macaroni

Servings:6
Cooking Time:50 Minutes

Ingredients:

- 10 Kalamata olives
- 1 ½ lb elbow macaroni
- 2 red chili peppers, minced
- 1 garlic clove, minced
- 2 whole garlic cloves
- 2 tbsp fresh parsley, chopped
- 1 ¼ cups fresh basil, sliced
- ½ cup extra-virgin olive oil
- ½ tsp honey
- ½ lemon, juiced and zested
- ¼ cup butter
- 1 small red onion, chopped
- 1 lb button mushrooms, sliced
- 1 tsp sweet paprika
- 6 ripe plum tomatoes, puréed
- ¼ cup dry white wine
- 1 oz ouzo
- 1 cup heavy cream
- 1 cup feta cheese, crumbled
- 24 shrimp, peeled and deveined
- 1 cup feta cheese, cubed
- 1 tsp dried Greek oregano
- Salt and black pepper to taste

Directions:

1. Bring to a boil salted water in a pot over high heat. Add the macaroni and cook for 6-8 minutes until al dente. Drain. Set aside. Preheat your broiler. Place the chilies, whole garlic, parsley, ¼ cup of basil, ¼ cup of oil, honey, lemon juice, lemon zest, and salt in a food processor and blend until all the ingredients are well incorporated. Set aside.

2. Warm the remaining olive oil and butter in a large skillet over medium heat. Sauté the onion, minced garlic, mushrooms, and paprika for 5 minutes until tender. Pour in the tomatoes, wine, and ouzo and season with salt and pepper. Simmer for 6–7 minutes until most of the liquid evaporates, 5 minutes.

3. Stir in the heavy cream and crumbled feta cheese for 3 minutes until the sauce is thickened. Add in remaining basil and pasta and stir to combine. Pour the mixture into a baking dish and top with shrimp and cubed feta cheese. Broil 5 minutes or until the shrimp turn pink and cheese melts. Drizzle with reserved parsley-basil sauce and sprinkle with oregano. Let cool for 5 minutes. Serve topped with olives.

Nutrition Info:

- Info Per Serving: Calories: 1004;Fat: 47g;Protein: 47g;Carbs: 97g.

Classic Garidomakaronada (shrimp & Pasta)

Servings:4
Cooking Time:45 Minutes
Ingredients:
- 2 tbsp olive oil
- 16 medium shrimp, shelled and deveined
- Salt and black pepper to taste
- 1 onion, finely chopped
- 3 garlic cloves, minced
- 4 tomatoes, puréed
- ½ tsp sugar
- 1 tbsp tomato paste
- 1 tbsp ouzo
- 1 lb whole-wheat spaghetti
- ½ tsp crushed red pepper
- ¼ tsp dried Greek oregano
- 2 tbsp chopped fresh parsley

Directions:

1. Bring a large pot of salted water to a boil, add the spaghetti, and cook for 7-9 minutes until al dente. Drain the pasta and set aside. Warm the olive oil in a large skillet over medium heat. Sauté the shrimp for 2 minutes, flipping once or until pink; set aside. Add the onion and garlic to the skillet and cook for 3-5 minutes or until tender.

2. Add tomatoes, sugar, oregano, and tomato paste. Bring the sauce to a boil. Reduce the heat and simmer for 15–20 minutes or until thickened. Stir in ouzo and season with salt and black pepper. Add the pasta along with crushed red pepper and cooked shrimp. Remove from heat and toss to coat the pasta. Sprinkle with parsley and serve immediately.

Nutrition Info:
- Info Per Serving: Calories: 319;Fat: 9g;Protein: 10g;Carbs: 51g.

Rice & Lentil Salad With Caramelized Onions

Servings:4
Cooking Time:1 Hour 15 Minutes
Ingredients:
- ¼ cup olive oil
- 2 cups lentils
- 1 cup brown rice
- 4 ½ cups water
- ½ tsp dried thyme
- ½ tsp dried tarragon
- 3 onions, peeled and sliced
- Salt and black pepper to taste

Directions:

1. Place the lentils and rice in a large saucepan with water. Bring to a boil, cover, and simmer for 23 minutes or until almost tender. Stir in the seasonings and cook for 25-30 minutes or until the rice is tender and the water is absorbed.

2. In a separate saucepan, warm the olive oil over medium heat. Add the onions and cook slowly, stirring frequently, until the onions brown and caramelize, for 17-20 minutes. Top with the caramelized onions. Serve and enjoy!

Nutrition Info:
- Info Per Serving: Calories: 498;Fat: 19g;Protein: 15g;Carbs: 63g.

Genovese Mussel Linguine

Servings:4
Cooking Time:40 Minutes

Ingredients:

- 1 lb mussels, scrubbed and debearded
- 1 tbsp olive oil
- ½ cup Pinot Grigio wine
- 2 garlic cloves, minced
- ½ tsp red pepper flakes
- ½ lemon, zested and juiced
- 1 lb linguine
- Salt and black pepper to taste
- 2 tbsp parsley, finely chopped

Directions:

1. In a saucepan, bring mussels and wine to a boil, cover, and cook, shaking pan occasionally, until mussels open, 5-7 minutes. As they open, remove them with a slotted spoon into a bowl. Discard all closed mussels. Drain steaming liquid through fine-mesh strainer into a bowl, avoiding any gritty sediment that has settled on the bottom of the pan.

2. Wipe the pan clean. Warm the olive oil in the pan and stir-fry garlic and pepper flake until the garlic turn golden, 3 minutes. Stir in reserved mussel liquid and lemon zest and juice, bring to a simmer and cook for 3-4 minutes. Stir in mussels and cook until heated through, 3 minutes.

3. Bring a large pot filled with salted water to a boil. Add pasta and cook until al dente. Reserve ½ cup of cooking liquid, drain pasta and return it to pot. Add the sauce and parsley and toss to combine and season to taste. Adjust consistency with the reserved cooking liquid as needed and serve.

Nutrition Info:

- Info Per Serving: Calories: 423;Fat: 9g;Protein: 16g;Carbs: 37g.

Authentic Fava Bean & Garbanzo Fül

Servings:6
Cooking Time:20 Minutes

Ingredients:

- 3 tbsp extra-virgin olive oil
- 1 can garbanzo beans
- 1 can fava beans
- ½ tsp lemon zest
- ½ tsp dried oregano
- ½ cup lemon juice
- 3 cloves garlic, minced
- Salt to taste

Directions:

1. Place the garbanzo beans, fava beans, and 3 cups of water in a pot over medium heat. Cook for 10 minutes. Drain the beans Reserving 1 cup of the liquid, and put them in a bowl. Mix the reserved liquid, lemon juice, lemon zest, oregano, minced garlic, and salt together and add to the beans in the bowl. With a potato masher, mash up about half the beans in the bowl. Stir the mixture to combine. Drizzle the olive oil over the top. Serve with pita bread if desired.

Nutrition Info:

- Info Per Serving: Calories: 199;Fat: 9g;Protein: 10g;Carbs: 25g.

Rich Cauliflower Alfredo

Servings:4
Cooking Time: 30 Minutes
Ingredients:

- Cauliflower Alfredo Sauce:
- 1 tablespoon avocado oil
- ½ yellow onion, diced
- 2 cups cauliflower florets
- 2 garlic cloves, minced
- 1½ teaspoons miso
- 1 teaspoon Dijon mustard
- Pinch of ground nutmeg
- ½ cup unsweetened almond milk
- 1½ tablespoons fresh lemon juice
- 2 tablespoons nutritional yeast
- Sea salt and ground black pepper, to taste
- Fettuccine:
- 1 tablespoon avocado oil
- ½ yellow onion, diced
- 1 cup broccoli florets
- 1 zucchini, halved lengthwise and cut into ¼-inch-thick half-moons
- Sea salt and ground black pepper, to taste
- ½ cup sun-dried tomatoes, drained if packed in oil
- 8 ounces cooked whole-wheat fettuccine
- ½ cup fresh basil, cut into ribbons

Directions:

1. Make the Sauce:
2. Heat the avocado oil in a nonstick skillet over medium-high heat until shimmering.
3. Add half of the onion to the skillet and sauté for 5 minutes or until translucent.
4. Add the cauliflower and garlic to the skillet. Reduce the heat to low and cook for 8 minutes or until the cauliflower is tender.
5. Pour them in a food processor, add the remaining ingredients for the sauce and pulse to combine well. Set aside.
6. Make the Fettuccine:
7. Heat the avocado oil in a nonstick skillet over medium-high heat.
8. Add the remaining half of onion and sauté for 5 minutes or until translucent.
9. Add the broccoli and zucchini. Sprinkle with salt and ground black pepper, then sauté for 5 minutes or until tender.
10. Add the sun-dried tomatoes, reserved sauce, and fettuccine. Sauté for 3 minutes or until well-coated and heated through.
11. Serve the fettuccine on a large plate and spread with basil before serving.

Nutrition Info:

- Info Per Serving: Calories: 288;Fat: 15.9g;Protein: 10.1g;Carbs: 32.5g.

Rosemary Fava Bean Purée

Servings:4
Cooking Time:20 Minutes
Ingredients:

- 3 tbsp olive oil
- 4 garlic cloves, minced
- 1 tsp ground cumin
- 2 cans fava beans
- 3 tbsp tahini
- 2 tbsp lemon juice
- 4 lemon wedges
- Salt and black pepper to taste
- 1 tomato, chopped
- 1 small onion, chopped
- 2 hard-cooked eggs, chopped
- 1 tbsp rosemary, chopped

Directions:

1. Warm 2 tbsp of olive oil in a saucepan over medium heat. Cook garlic cumin until fragrant, about 2 minutes. Stir in beans and their liquid and tahini. Bring to a simmer and cook until liquid thickens slightly, 8-10 minutes. Heat off.
2. Mash beans to a coarse consistency using a potato masher. Stir in lemon juice. Season with salt and pepper. Top with tomato, onion, rosemary, and eggs, and drizzle with the remaining oil. Serve with lemon wedges.

Nutrition Info:

- Info Per Serving: Calories: 173;Fat: 8.8g;Protein: 9g;Carbs: 9.8g.

Fruits, Desserts And Snacks Recipes

Speedy Trail Mix

Servings:6
Cooking Time:10 Minutes
Ingredients:

- ½ cup chopped macadamia
- ½ cup chopped walnuts
- ½ cup chopped salted almonds
- ½ cup shelled salted pistachios
- ½ cup chopped apricots
- ½ cup chopped dates
- ⅓ cup dried figs, halved

Directions:

1. Place all the nuts in a skillet over medium heat and toast them for 2 minutes, shaking often. Remove and leave them to cool completely. Mix with the apricots, dates, and figs. Serve.

Nutrition Info:

- Info Per Serving: Calories: 348;Fat: 24g;Protein: 9g;Carbs: 33g.

Roasted Carrot Ribbons With Mayo Sauce

Servings:4
Cooking Time:50 Minutes
Ingredients:

- 2 tbsp olive oil
- 1 lb carrots, shaved into ribbons
- Salt and black pepper to taste
- ½ lemon, zested
- 1/3 cup light mayonnaise
- 1 garlic clove, minced
- 1 tsp cumin, ground
- 1 tbsp dill, chopped

Directions:

1. Preheat the oven to 380 F. Spread carrot ribbons on a paper-lined roasting tray. Drizzle with some olive oil and sprinkle with cumin, salt, and pepper. Roast for 20-25 minutes until crisp and golden. In a bowl, mix mayonnaise, lemon zest, garlic, dill, and remaining olive oil. Serve the roasted carrots with mayo sauce.

Nutrition Info:

- Info Per Serving: Calories: 200;Fat: 6g;Protein: 6g;Carbs: 8g.

Stuffed Cherry Tomatoes

Servings:4
Cooking Time:10 Minutes
Ingredients:

- 2 tbsp olive oil
- 16 cherry tomatoes
- 1 tbsp lemon zest
- ½ cup feta cheese, crumbled
- 2 tbsp olive tapenade
- ¼ cup parsley, torn

Directions:

1. Using a sharp knife, slice off the tops of the tomatoes and hollow out the insides. Combine olive oil, lemon zest, feta cheese, olive tapenade, and parsley in a bowl. Fill the cherry tomatoes with the feta mixture and arrange them on a plate.

Nutrition Info:

- Info Per Serving: Calories: 140;Fat: 9g;Protein: 6g;Carbs: 6g.

Orange Mug Cakes

Servings:2
Cooking Time: 3 Minutes

Ingredients:

- 6 tablespoons flour
- 2 tablespoons sugar
- 1 teaspoon orange zest
- ½ teaspoon baking powder
- Pinch salt
- 1 egg
- 2 tablespoons olive oil
- 2 tablespoons unsweetened almond milk
- 2 tablespoons freshly squeezed orange juice
- ½ teaspoon orange extract
- ½ teaspoon vanilla extract

Directions:

1. Combine the flour, sugar, orange zest, baking powder, and salt in a small bowl.
2. In another bowl, whisk together the egg, olive oil, milk, orange juice, orange extract, and vanilla extract.
3. Add the dry ingredients to the wet ingredients and stir to incorporate. The batter will be thick.
4. Divide the mixture into two small mugs. Microwave each mug separately. The small ones should take about 60 seconds, and one large mug should take about 90 seconds, but microwaves can vary.
5. Cool for 5 minutes before serving.

Nutrition Info:

- Info Per Serving: Calories: 303;Fat: 16.9g;Protein: 6.0g;Carbs: 32.5g.

Baked Beet Fries With Feta Cheese

Servings:4
Cooking Time:40 Minutes

Ingredients:

- 1 cup olive oil
- 1 cup feta cheese, crumbled
- 2 beets, sliced
- Salt and black pepper to taste
- 1/3 cup balsamic vinegar

Directions:

1. Preheat the oven to 340 F. Line a baking sheet with parchment paper. Arrange beet slices, salt, pepper, vinegar, and olive oil on the sheet and toss to combine. Bake for 30 minutes. Serve topped with feta cheese.

Nutrition Info:

- Info Per Serving: Calories: 210;Fat: 6g;Protein: 4g;Carbs: 9g.

Simple Peanut Butter And Chocolate Balls

Servings:15
Cooking Time: 0 Minutes

Ingredients:

- ¾ cup creamy peanut butter
- ¼ cup unsweetened cocoa powder
- 2 tablespoons softened almond butter
- ½ teaspoon vanilla extract
- 1¾ cups maple sugar

Directions:

1. Line a baking sheet with parchment paper.
2. Combine all the ingredients in a bowl. Stir to mix well.
3. Divide the mixture into 15 parts and shape each part into a 1-inch ball.
4. Arrange the balls on the baking sheet and refrigerate for at least 30 minutes, then serve chilled.

Nutrition Info:

- Info Per Serving: Calories: 146;Fat: 8.1g;Protein: 4.2g;Carbs: 16.9g.

Salty Spicy Popcorn

Servings:6
Cooking Time:10 Minutes
Ingredients:

- 3 tbsp olive oil
- ¼ tsp garlic powder
- Salt and black pepper to taste
- ½ tsp dried thyme
- ½ tsp chili powder
- ½ tsp dried oregano
- 12 cups plain popped popcorn

Directions:

1. Warm the olive oil in a large pan over medium heat. Add the garlic powder, black pepper, salt, chili powder, thyme, and stir oregano until fragrant, 1 minute. Place the popcorn in a large bowl and drizzle with the infused oil over. Toss to coat.

Nutrition Info:

- Info Per Serving: Calories: 183;Fat: 12g;Protein: 3g;Carbs: 19g.

Two-cheese & Spinach Pizza Bagels

Servings:6
Cooking Time:20 Minutes
Ingredients:

- 2 tbsp olive oil
- 6 bagels, halved and toasted
- 2 green onions, chopped
- 1 cup pizza sauce
- ¼ tsp dried oregano
- 1 cup spinach, torn
- 1 ¼ cups mozzarella, grated
- ¼ cup Parmesan cheese, grated

Directions:

1. Preheat your broiler. Arrange the bagels on a baking sheet. Warm the olive oil in a saucepan over medium heat and sauté the green onions for 3-4 minutes until tender. Pour in the pizza sauce and oregano and bring to a simmer.
2. Spread the bagel halves with the sauce mixture and top with spinach. Sprinkle with mozzarella and Parmesan cheeses. Place under the preheated broiler for 5-6 minutes or until the cheeses melt.

Nutrition Info:

- Info Per Serving: Calories: 366;Fat: 8g;Protein: 20g;Carbs: 55g.

Honey & Spice Roasted Almonds

Servings:4
Cooking Time:15 Minutes
Ingredients:

- 2 tbsp olive oil
- 3 cups almonds
- 1 tbsp curry powder
- ¼ cup honey
- 1 tsp salt

Directions:

1. Preheat oven to 260 F. Coat almonds with olive oil, curry powder, and salt in a bowl; mix well. Arrange on a lined with aluminum foil sheet and bake for 15 minutes. Remove from the oven and let cool for 10 minutes. Drizzle with honey and let cool at room temperature. Enjoy!

Nutrition Info:

- Info Per Serving: Calories: 134;Fat: 8g;Protein: 1g;Carbs: 18g.

Pizza A La Portuguesa

Servings:4
Cooking Time:35 Minutes
Ingredients:
- For the crust
- 2 tbsp olive oil
- 2 cups flour
- 1 cup lukewarm water
- 1 pinch of sugar
- 1 tsp active dry yeast
- ¾ tsp salt
- For the topping
- 2 tbsp pizza sauce
- 2 red onions, thinly sliced
- 1 tsp dry oregano
- 2 cups shredded mozzarella
- 2 boiled eggs thinly sliced
- 12 green olives

Directions:
1. Sift the flour and salt in a bowl and stir in yeast. Mix lukewarm water, olive oil, and sugar in another bowl. Add the wet mixture to the dry mixture and whisk until you obtain a soft dough. Place the dough on a floured work surface and knead it thoroughly for 4-5 minutes until elastic. Transfer the dough to a greased bowl. Cover with cling film and leave to rise for 50-60 minutes in a warm place until doubled in size. Roll out the dough to a thickness of around 12 inches. Place on a pizza pan covered with parchment paper
2. Preheat the oven to 450 F. Spread the pizza sauce on the crust. Sprinkle with oregano, then mozzarella cheese, then the onions, and finally the olives. Bake in the oven for 10 minutes. Top with eggs and serve sliced into wedges..

Nutrition Info:
- Info Per Serving: Calories: 317;Fat: 20g;Protein: 28g;Carbs: 1g.

Balsamic Strawberry Caprese Skewers

Servings:6
Cooking Time:15 Min + Cooling Time
Ingredients:
- 1 tbsp olive oil
- 1 cup balsamic vinegar
- 24 whole, hulled strawberries
- 24 basil leaves, halved
- 12 fresh mozzarella balls

Directions:
1. Pour the balsamic vinegar into a small saucepan and simmer for 10 minutes or until it's reduced by half and is thick enough to coat the back of a spoon. Set aside to cool completely. Thread the strawberries onto wooden skewers, followed by basil leaves folded in half and mozzarella balls. Drizzle with balsamic glaze and olive oil and serve.

Nutrition Info:
- Info Per Serving: Calories: 206;Fat: 10g;Protein: 10g;Carbs: 17g.

Mint Banana Chocolate Sorbet

Servings:1

Cooking Time: 0 Minutes

Ingredients:

- 1 frozen banana
- 1 tablespoon almond butter
- 2 tablespoons minced fresh mint
- 2 to 3 tablespoons dark chocolate chips
- 2 to 3 tablespoons goji (optional)

Directions:

1. Put the banana, butter, and mint in a food processor. Pulse to purée until creamy and smooth.
2. Add the chocolate and goji, then pulse for several more times to combine well.
3. Pour the mixture in a bowl or a ramekin, then freeze for at least 4 hours before serving chilled.

Nutrition Info:

- Info Per Serving: Calories: 213;Fat: 9.8g;Protein: 3.1g;Carbs: 2.9g.

Glazed Pears With Hazelnuts

Servings:4

Cooking Time: 20 Minutes

Ingredients:

- 4 pears, peeled, cored, and quartered lengthwise
- 1 cup apple juice
- 1 tablespoon grated fresh ginger
- ½ cup pure maple syrup
- ¼ cup chopped hazelnuts

Directions:

1. Put the pears in a pot, then pour in the apple juice. Bring to a boil over medium-high heat, then reduce the heat to medium-low. Stir constantly.
2. Cover and simmer for an additional 15 minutes or until the pears are tender.
3. Meanwhile, combine the ginger and maple syrup in a saucepan. Bring to a boil over medium-high heat. Stir frequently. Turn off the heat and transfer the syrup to a small bowl and let sit until ready to use.
4. Transfer the pears in a large serving bowl with a slotted spoon, then top the pears with syrup.
5. Spread the hazelnuts over the pears and serve immediately.

Nutrition Info:

- Info Per Serving: Calories: 287;Fat: 3.1g;Protein: 2.2g;Carbs: 66.9g.

Garlic-yogurt Dip With Walnuts

Servings:4

Cooking Time:5 Minutes

Ingredients:

- 2 cups Greek yogurt
- 3 garlic cloves, minced
- ¼ cup dill, chopped
- 1 green onion, chopped
- ¼ cup walnuts, chopped
- Salt and black pepper to taste

Directions:

1. Combine garlic, yogurt, dill, walnuts, salt, and pepper in a bowl. Serve topped with green onion.

Nutrition Info:

- Info Per Serving: Calories: 210;Fat: 7g;Protein: 9g;Carbs: 16g.

Lamb Ragu Tagliatelle

Servings:4

Cooking Time:25 Minutes

Ingredients:

- 2 tbsp olive oil
- 16 oz tagliatelle
- 1 tsp paprika
- 1 tsp cumin
- Salt and black pepper to taste
- 1 lb ground lamb
- 1 cup onions, chopped
- ¼ cup parsley, chopped
- 2 garlic cloves, minced

Directions:

1. Boil the tagliatelle in a pot over medium heat for 9-11 minutes or until "al dente". Drain and set aside.

2. Warm the olive oil in a skillet over medium heat and sauté lamb, onions, and garlic until the meat is browned, about 10-15 minutes. Stir in cumin, paprika, salt, and pepper for 1-2 minutes. Spoon tagliatelle on a platter and scatter lamb over. Top with parsley and serve.

Nutrition Info:

- Info Per Serving: Calories: 140;Fat: 10g;Protein: 6g;Carbs: 7g.

Baby Artichoke Antipasto

Servings:4

Cooking Time:5 Minutes

Ingredients:

- 1 jar roasted red peppers
- 8 canned artichoke hearts
- 1 can garbanzo beans
- 1 cup whole Kalamata olives
- ¼ cup balsamic vinegar
- Salt to taste
- 1 lemon, zested

Directions:

1. Slice the peppers and put them into a large bowl. Cut the artichoke hearts into quarters, and add them to the bowl. Add the garbanzo beans, olives, balsamic vinegar, lemon zest, and salt. Toss all the ingredients together. Serve chilled.

Nutrition Info:

- Info Per Serving: Calories: 281;Fat: 15g;Protein: 7g;Carbs: 30g.

Lebanese Spicy Baba Ganoush

Servings:4

Cooking Time:50 Minutes

Ingredients:

- 2 tbsp olive oil
- 2 eggplants, poked with a fork
- 2 tbsp tahini paste
- 1 tsp cayenne pepper
- 2 tbsp lemon juice
- 2 garlic cloves, minced
- Salt and black pepper to taste
- 1 tbsp parsley, chopped

Directions:

1. Preheat oven to 380 F. Arrange eggplants on a roasting pan and bake for 40 minutes. Set aside to cool. Peel the cooled eggplants and place them in a blender along with the tahini paste, lemon juice, garlic, cayenne pepper, salt, and pepper. Puree the ingredients while gradually adding olive oil until a smooth and homogeneous consistency. Top with parsley.

Nutrition Info:

- Info Per Serving: Calories: 130;Fat: 5g;Protein: 5g;Carbs: 2g.

Cherry Walnut Brownies

Servings:9

Cooking Time: 20 Minutes

Ingredients:

- 2 large eggs
- ½ cup 2% plain Greek yogurt
- ½ cup sugar
- ⅓ cup honey
- ¼ cup extra-virgin olive oil
- 1 teaspoon vanilla extract
- ½ cup whole-wheat pastry flour
- ⅓ cup unsweetened dark chocolate cocoa powder
- ¼ teaspoon baking powder
- ¼ teaspoon salt
- ⅓ cup chopped walnuts
- 9 fresh cherries, stemmed and pitted
- Cooking spray

Directions:

1. Preheat the oven to 375ºF and set the rack in the middle of the oven. Spritz a square baking pan with cooking spray.

2. In a large bowl, whisk together the eggs, yogurt, sugar, honey, oil and vanilla.

3. In a medium bowl, stir together the flour, cocoa powder, baking powder and salt. Add the flour mixture to the egg mixture and whisk until all the dry ingredients are incorporated. Fold in the walnuts.

4. Pour the batter into the prepared pan. Push the cherries into the batter, three to a row in three rows, so one will be at the center of each brownie once you cut them into squares.

5. Bake the brownies for 20 minutes, or until just set. Remove from the oven and place on a rack to cool for 5 minutes. Cut into nine squares and serve.

Nutrition Info:

- Info Per Serving: Calories: 154;Fat: 6.0g;Protein: 3.0g;Carbs: 24.0g.

Parsley Roasted Pepper Hummus

Servings:6

Cooking Time:10 Minutes

Ingredients:

- 6 oz roasted red peppers, chopped
- 4 tbsp olive oil
- 16 oz canned chickpeas
- ¼ cup mayonnaise
- 3 tbsp tahini paste
- 1 lemon, juiced
- 3 garlic cloves, minced
- Salt and black pepper to taste
- 1 tbsp parsley, chopped

Directions:

1. In a blender, pulse red peppers, chickpeas, mayonnaise, tahini paste, lemon juice, garlic, salt, and pepper until you obtain a smooth mixture. Continue blending while gradually adding olive oil until smooth. Serve sprinkled with parsley.

Nutrition Info:

- Info Per Serving: Calories: 260;Fat: 12g;Protein: 7g;Carbs: 18g.

Two Cheese Pizza

Servings:4
Cooking Time:35 Minutes
Ingredients:
- For the crust:
- 1 tbsp olive oil
- ½ cup almond flour
- ¼ tsp salt
- 2 tbsp ground psyllium husk
- For the topping
- ½ cup pizza sauce
- 4 oz mozzarella, sliced
- 1 cup grated mozzarella
- 3 tbsp grated Parmesan cheese
- 2 tsp Italian seasoning

Directions:
1. Preheat the oven to 400 F. Line a baking sheet with parchment paper. In a medium bowl, mix the almond flour, salt, psyllium powder, olive oil, and 1 cup of lukewarm water until dough forms. Spread the mixture on the pizza pan and bake in the oven until crusty, 10 minutes. When ready, remove the crust and spread the pizza sauce on top. Add the sliced mozzarella, grated mozzarella, Parmesan cheese, and Italian seasoning. Bake in the oven for 18 minutes or until the cheeses melt. Serve warm.

Nutrition Info:
- Info Per Serving: Calories: 193;Fat: 10g;Protein: 19g;Carbs: 3g.

Pomegranate Blueberry Granita

Servings:2
Cooking Time:15 Min + Freezing Time
Ingredients:
- 1 cup blueberries
- 1 cup pomegranate juice
- ¼ cup sugar
- ¼ tsp lemon zest

Directions:
1. Place the blueberries, lemon zest, and pomegranate juice in a saucepan over medium heat and bring to a boil. Simmer for 5 minutes or until the blueberries start to break down. Stir the sugar in ¼ cup of water until the sugar is dissolved. Place the blueberry mixture and the sugar water in your blender and blitz for 1 minute or until the fruit is puréed.
2. Pour the mixture into a baking pan. The liquid should come about ½ inch up the sides. Let the mixture cool for 30 minutes, and then put it into the freezer. Every 30 minutes for the next 2 hours, scrape the granita with a fork to keep it from freezing solid. Serve it after 2 hours, or store it in a covered container in the freezer.

Nutrition Info:
- Info Per Serving: Calories: 214;Fat: 0g;Protein: 1g;Carbs: 54g.

Fruit And Nut Chocolate Bark

Servings:2
Cooking Time: 2 Minutes
Ingredients:

- 2 tablespoons chopped nuts
- 3 ounces dark chocolate chips
- ¼ cup chopped dried fruit (blueberries, apricots, figs, prunes, or any combination of those)

Directions:

1. Line a sheet pan with parchment paper and set aside.
2. Add the nuts to a skillet over medium-high heat and toast for 60 seconds, or just fragrant. Set aside to cool.
3. Put the chocolate chips in a microwave-safe glass bowl and microwave on High for 1 minute.
4. Stir the chocolate and allow any unmelted chips to warm and melt. If desired, heat for an additional 20 to 30 seconds.
5. Transfer the chocolate to the prepared sheet pan. Scatter the dried fruit and toasted nuts over the chocolate evenly and gently pat in so they stick.
6. Place the sheet pan in the refrigerator for at least 1 hour to let the chocolate harden.
7. When ready, break into pieces and serve.

Nutrition Info:

- Info Per Serving: Calories: 285;Fat: 16.1g;Protein: 4.0g;Carbs: 38.7g.

Greek Yogurt & Za'atar Dip On Grilled Pitta

Servings:6
Cooking Time:10 Minutes
Ingredients:

- 1/3 cup olive oil
- 2 cups Greek yogurt
- 2 tbsp toasted ground pistachios
- Salt and white pepper to taste
- 2 tbsp mint, chopped
- 3 kalamata olives, chopped
- ¼ cup za'atar seasoning
- 3 pitta breads, cut into triangles

Directions:

1. Mix the yogurt, pistachios, salt, pepper, mint, olives, za´atar spice, and olive oil in a bowl. Grill the pitta bread until golden, about 5-6 minutes. Serve with the yogurt spread.

Nutrition Info:

- Info Per Serving: Calories: 300;Fat: 19g;Protein: 11g;Carbs: 22g.

Dark Chocolate Barks

Servings:6
Cooking Time:20 Min + Freezing Time
Ingredients:

- ½ cup quinoa
- ½ tsp sea salt
- 1 cup dark chocolate chips
- ½ tsp mint extract
- ½ cup pomegranate seeds

Directions:

1. Toast the quinoa in a greased saucepan for 2-3 minutes, stirring frequently. Remove the pan from the stove and mix in the salt. Set aside 2 tablespoons of the toasted quinoa.
2. Microwave the chocolate for 1 minute. Stir until the chocolate is completely melted. Mix the toasted quinoa and mint extract into the melted chocolate. Line a large, rimmed baking sheet with parchment paper. Spread the chocolate mixture onto the sheet. Sprinkle the remaining 2 tablespoons of quinoa and pomegranate seeds, pressing with a spatula. Freeze the mixture for 10-15 minutes or until set. Remove and break into about 2-inch jagged pieces. Store in the refrigerator until ready to serve.

Nutrition Info:

- Info Per Serving: Calories: 268;Fat: 12g;Protein: 4g;Carbs: 37g.

Artichoke & Sun-dried Tomato Pizza

Servings:4
Cooking Time:80 Minutes
Ingredients:

- 2 tbsp olive oil
- 1 cup canned passata
- 2 cups flour
- 1 pinch of sugar
- 1 tsp active dry yeast
- ¾ tsp salt
- 1 ½ cups artichoke hearts
- ¼ cup grated Asiago cheese
- ½ onion, minced
- 3 garlic cloves, minced
- 1 tbsp dried oregano
- 6 sundried tomatoes, chopped
- ½ tsp red pepper flakes
- 5-6 basil leaves, torn

Directions:

1. Sift the flour and salt in a bowl and stir in yeast. Mix 1 cup of lukewarm water, olive oil, and sugar in another bowl. Add the wet mixture to the dry mixture and whisk until you obtain a soft dough. Place the dough on a lightly floured work surface and knead it thoroughly for 4-5 minutes until elastic. Transfer the dough to a greased bowl. Cover with cling film and leave to rise for 50-60 minutes in a warm place until doubled in size. Roll out the dough to a thickness of around 12 inches.

2. Preheat oven to 400 F. Warm oil in a saucepan over medium heat and sauté onion and garlic for 3-4 minutes. Mix in tomatoes and oregano and bring to a boil. Decrease the heat and simmer for another 5 minutes. Transfer the pizza crust to a baking sheet. Spread the sauce all over and top with artichoke hearts and sun-dried tomatoes. Scatter the cheese and bake for 15 minutes until golden. Top with red pepper flakes and basil leaves and serve sliced.

Nutrition Info:

- Info Per Serving: Calories: 254;Fat: 9.5g;Protein: 8g;Carbs: 34.3g.

Wrapped Pears In Prosciutto

Servings:4
Cooking Time:5 Minutes
Ingredients:

- 2 pears, cored and cut into wedges
- 4 oz prosciutto slices, halved lengthwise
- 1 tbsp chives, chopped
- 1 tsp red pepper flakes

Directions:

1. Wrap the pear wedges with prosciutto slices. Transfer them to a platter. Garnish with chives and pepper flakes. Serve.

Nutrition Info:

- Info Per Serving: Calories: 35;Fat: 2g;Protein: 12g;Carbs: 5g.

Appendix : Recipes Index

Chicken And Pastina Soup 52
Chicken With Chianti Sauce 22
Chickpea Lettuce Wraps 7
Chili & Cheese Frittata 13
Chili Flounder Parcels 28
Cilantro Turkey Penne With Asparagus 24
Classic Garidomakaronada (shrimp & Pasta) 72
Classic Zuppa Toscana 56
Cocktail Meatballs In Almond Sauce 24
Creamy Breakfast Bulgur With Berries 16
Creamy Cauliflower Chickpea Curry 42
Creamy Peach Smoothie 15
Creamy Saffron Chicken With Ziti 67
Creamy Trout Spread 28
Creamy Vanilla Oatmeal 9
Crispy Herb Crusted Halibut 31
Cumin Rice Stuffed Bell Peppers 70

D

Dark Chocolate Barks 83
Dill Baked Sea Bass 36
Dulse, Avocado, And Tomato Pitas 7

E

Easy Pork Stew 18
Easy Romesco Sauce 54
Easy Simple Pesto Pasta 67
Egg & Spinach Pie 14
Eggplant & Sweet Potato Salad 51
Exotic Pork Chops 19

F

Fancy Turkish Salad 56
Farro & Trout Bowls With Avocado 30
Favorite Green Bean Stir-fry 53
Fresh Mozzarella & Salmon Frittata 6
Fried Eggplant Rolls 40
Fried Scallops With Bean Mash 32
Fruit And Nut Chocolate Bark 83

G

Garlic And Parsley Chickpeas 68
Garlic Herb Butter 55
Garlicky Beef With Walnuts 27
Garlic-yogurt Dip With Walnuts 79
Genovese Mussel Linguine 73
Glazed Pears With Hazelnuts 79
Gorgonzola, Fig & Prosciutto Salad 60
Greek Yogurt & Za'atar Dip On Grilled Pitta 83
Greek-style Chicken With Potatoes 25

Greek-style Shrimp & Feta Macaroni 71
Grilled Romaine Lettuce 41
Grilled Sardines With Herby Sauce 33

H

Harissa Turkey With Couscous 17
Homemade Herbes De Provence Spice 58
Honey & Spice Roasted Almonds 77
Honey-mustard Roasted Salmon 34
Hot Collard Green Oats With Parmesan 62

I

Italian Tarragon Buckwheat 66

J

Jalapeño Veggie Rice Stew 71

L

Lamb Ragu Tagliatelle 80
Lamb With Couscous & Chickpeas 20
Lebanese Flavor Broken Thin Noodles 66
Lebanese Spicy Baba Ganoush 80
Lemon Rosemary Roasted Branzino 37
Lemony Trout With Caramelized Shallots 33

M

Mediterranean Eggs (shakshuka) 9
Mediterranean Grilled Sea Bass 35
Mediterranean-style Beans And Greens 63
Mint Banana Chocolate Sorbet 79
Minty Broccoli & Walnuts 40
Morning Baklava French Toast 12
Moroccan Tagine With Vegetables 46
Mushroom & Parmesan Risotto 57
Mushroom-barley Soup 57

O

One-bowl Microwave Lasagna 69
Orange Mug Cakes 76
Oven-baked Spanish Salmon 38

P

Parmesan Asparagus With Tomatoes 44
Parmesan Stuffed Zucchini Boats 47
Parsley Roasted Pepper Hummus 81
Parsley Salmon Bake 34
Parsley-dijon Chicken And Potatoes 19

Picante Beef Stew 22
Pizza A La Portuguesa 78
Pomegranate Blueberry Granita 82
Pork Chops With Squash & Zucchini 26

Q

Quick Steamed Broccoli 45
Quinoa & Chicken Bowl 23

R

Restaurant-style Zuppa Di Fagioli 60
Ribollita (tuscan Bean Soup) 68
Rice & Lentil Salad With Caramelized Onions 72
Rich Beef Meal 18
Rich Cauliflower Alfredo 74
Roasted Caramelized Root Vegetables 45
Roasted Carrot Ribbons With Mayo Sauce 75
Roasted Celery Root With Yogurt Sauce 43
Roasted Root Vegetable Soup 55
Roasted Vegetables 46
Rosemary Fava Bean Purée 74
Rosemary Pork Loin With Green Onions 17
Rosemary Tomato Chicken 18

S

Salmon Stuffed Peppers 29
Salty Spicy Popcorn 77
Saucy Turkey With Ricotta Cheese 24
Sautéed Cabbage With Parsley 49
Seafood Cakes With Radicchio Salad 35
Shrimp & Salmon In Tomato Sauce 36
Shrimp & Spinach A La Puttanesca 31
Simple Honey-glazed Baby Carrots 39
Simple Peanut Butter And Chocolate Balls 76
Spanish-style Green Beans With Pine Nuts 43
Speedy Trail Mix 75
Spiced Beef Meatballs 26
Spicy Cod Fillets 38
Spicy Potato Wedges 47
Spicy Roasted Tomatoes 44
Spinach & Lentil Stew 49
Spinach & Salmon Fettuccine In White Sauce 65
Spinach Farfalle With Ricotta Cheese 70
Steamed Beetroot With Nutty Yogurt 42
Stuffed Cherry Tomatoes 75
Sun-dried Tomato & Spinach Pasta Salad 59
Sweet Banana Pancakes With Strawberries 14
Sweet Chicken Stew 22
Sweet Mustard Cabbage Hash 39
Sweet Pork Stew 25
Sweet Potato Chickpea Buddha Bowl 48

Syrupy Chicken Breasts 23

T
Tasty Beanballs In Marinara Sauce 64
Tomato & Spinach Egg Wraps 11
Tomatoes Filled With Tabbouleh 48
Tradicional Matchuba Green Beans 43
Traditional Dukkah Spice 51
Tuna Burgers 29
Tuna Gyros With Tzatziki 30
Turkish Chickpeas 58
Two Cheese Pizza 82
Two-cheese & Spinach Pizza Bagels 77

V
Valencian-style Mussel Rice 64
Veg Mix And Blackeye Pea Burritos 13
Vegetable Polenta With Fried Eggs 16
Veggie & Beef Ragu 62

W
Warm Kale Salad With Red Bell Pepper 58
Wild Rice With Cheese & Mushrooms 65
Wrapped Pears In Prosciutto 84

Y
Yogurt Cucumber Salad 54
Yummy Lentil Stuffed Pitas 11

Z
Za'atar Pizza 8
Zucchini Hummus Wraps 6

Printed in Great Britain
by Amazon

28013587R00057

Introduction

Music Theory Practice - Complete Course is an invaluable resource for those taking a Grade Music Theory Exam, Grades 1-5, at both ABRSM and Trinity College.

This book contains not only a detailed explanation of each topic, but practice questions complete with answers for you to test your understanding.

As a music teacher of over 35 years of experience, I have never had a student fail a theory exam. Through my own understanding of what works best for students and how some of the alternative material on the market can sometimes be a very tedious method of learning, I have developed this course as a compliment to my video series on the YouTube channel *MusicOnline UK* and I am confident that you will find success in your exam by going through this course.

PAST PAPER MARKING SERVICE

In addition to the exercises in this book you can make use of the Past Paper Marking Service - FREE to Patrons of MusicOnline UK, so that you can really understand how well you have mastered the various topics.

More details available on www.patreon.com/musiconlineuk

So are you ready to get started on your road to Music Theory understanding.....

Lesson 1.1 - Time values, bar lines and time signatures.

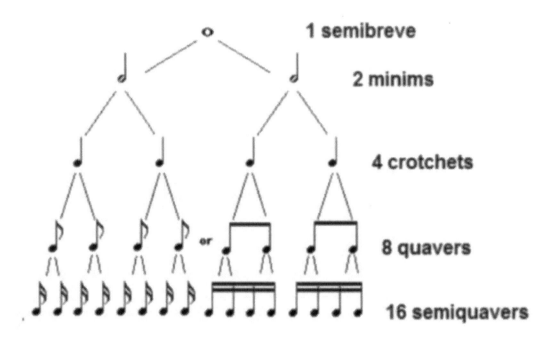

The above diagram shows that:

    1 semibreve is equal to
    2 minims, which are equal to
    4 crotchets, which are equal to
    8 quavers, which are equal to
    16 semiquavers.

The above stave contains three **Bars** separated by **Bar Lines.** At the end of the line there is a "**Double Bar Line**".

At the beginning of each bar there is a **Time Signature**. The top number of a time signature tells you **how many beats** are in a bar, and the bottom number tells you "**what type of beat it is**".

For example, in the first bar there is a time signature of 2/4.

This means that there are two beats in a bar and the beats are crotchets, or put more simply there are "two crotchet beats in bar".

The second bar has a time signature of 3/4 meaning "three crotchet beats in a bar". Notice that this doesn't necessarily mean three crotchets in that bar - it could be, as above, a minim and a crotchet which adds up to the same as three crotchet beats.

In the final bar there is a letter "C" which stands for "common time". Common time is just another way of writing 4/4 (i.e. four crotchet beats in a bar).

N.B. In Grade 1 you will only see time signatures with crotchet beats. In other words the bottom number of the time signature will always be 4 (or it's marked as common time which means 4/4).

Now try the worksheet on the next page to test your knowledge.

Questions

1. Write a time signature at the start of each of the following lines.

2. Add bar lines to the following.

3. Give the full meaning of 3/4 time.   3 beats in bar
                                           4 crotchets

4. How many semiquavers are worth the same as a minim?

$$\text{o} = 2 \times \text{o} = 2 \times (2 \times \text{o}) = 2 \times 2 \times 2 \times \text{o} = 8$$

5. What is another way of writing 4/4 time

(Answers to all worksheets are to be found at the end of this book)

Lesson 1.2 - Writing Notes on the Stave.

When drawing notes on the stave the main thing to remember for the purpose of examinations, (and for general practice) is that neatness is essential. In an examination marks will be lost for untidy work. With this in mind the following points should be noted.

Notes in spaces should fit exactly between the lines with no overlap.

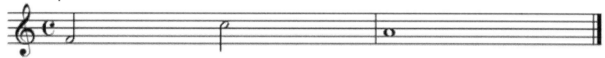

Notes on lines should have the line going through the middle of the note and occupy exactly half the spaces either side of the line.

The stems of high notes (above the middle line) go down on the left. The stems of low notes (below the middle line) go up on the right.

When drawing tails on the stems for quavers or semiquavers they always curve on the right hand side.

Questions

1. Turn these semibreves into crotchets by filling in the note heads and adding stems. *Be careful about the direction of the stems - whether they go up or down on the left or right.*

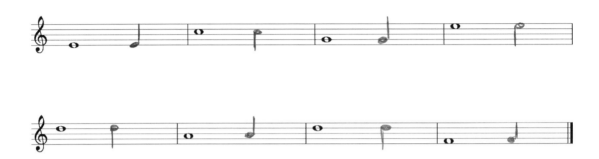

2. Now turn these notes into quavers by adding a curly tail. *Again be careful which side you add the tail.*

3. The following notes contain *four* deliberate mistakes. Circle the wrong notes and describe what is wrong with them.

Lesson 1.3 - Treble and Bass Clefs.

Before writing any notes in the treble clef you need to be able to draw the clef neatly for yourself. Bear in mind the following points:

Start around the 2nd line from the bottom and loop around clockwise so that your clef just touches the middle and bottom line. Then slant up to the top looping over just above the top of the stave. Bring an almost vertical line down the middle to finish just below the bottom of the stave.

The names of the notes in the *spaces* of the treble clef can easily be remembered using the word FACE

The names of the notes on the *lines* of the treble clef can likewise be remembered using the phrase "Every green bus drives fast"

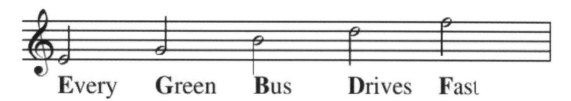

The drawing of a bass clef is somewhat easier than the treble clef. Nevertheless care must still be taken to make it neat.

The curve is tighter at the top than the bottom. The two dots after the bass clef must be in the top two spaces of the stave.

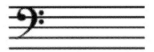

The names of the notes in the spaces of the bass clef can easily be remembered using the phrase "All Cows Eat Grass"

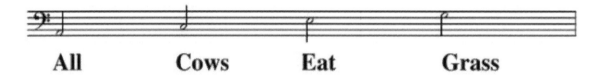

All   **Cows**   **Eat**   **Grass**

The names of the notes on the lines of the bass clef can likewise be remembered using the phrase "Grizzly Bears Don't Fear Anything"

Grizzly Bears   Don't   Fear   Anything

Questions

1. To start off, practice writing a row of treble clefs after the first example.

2. Name the notes below. Notice the clef keeps changing.

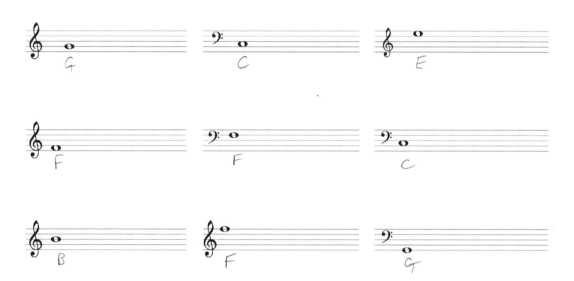

3. Insert either a treble or bass clef before each of these notes to make the letter names correct.

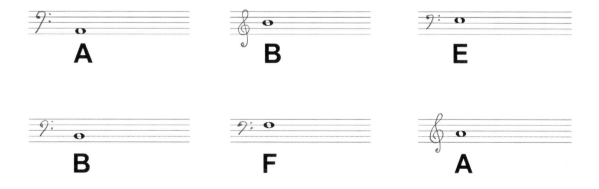

Lesson 1.4 - Beaming Notes

When quavers and semiquavers are written on their own, they have a small curly tail (or two - for semiquavers) to the right of the note stem. When they are joined together in groups, the 'curly tail' is replaced by a beam, or double beam for semiquavers.

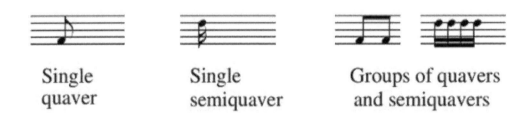

Single
quaver

Single
semiquaver

Groups of quavers
and semiquavers

Quavers and semiquavers can also be joined together in the same 'beam' as shown in the examples below.

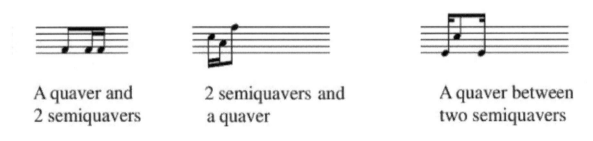

A quaver and
2 semiquavers

2 semiquavers and
a quaver

A quaver between
two semiquavers

Notice also the direction of the stems. The rules for this have been discussed in an earlier lesson, but when there is more than one note joined together in a beam some compromise needs to be found. If there is a majority, i.e. two go up and one down, then the majority wins (they all go up). If there is an even number, eg. two up two down then the ones furthest from the middle win.

2 up, 1 down = all up

The last 2 are further from the middle, so all 4 go down.

Questions

In each of the ***empty*** bars below copy the groups of quavers and/or semiquavers from each preceeding bar, but grouped together with a beam (or double beam in the case of semiquavers) as shown in the first example.

Example

Lesson 1.5 - Rests

All the time values for notes that you have learned, have corresponding signs for rests of the same value.

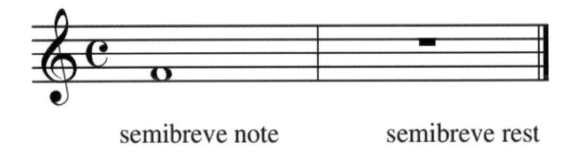

semibreve note   semibreve rest

Note: the semibreve rest is always used for a whole bar of rest whatever the time signature, 4/4, 3/4 or 2/4.

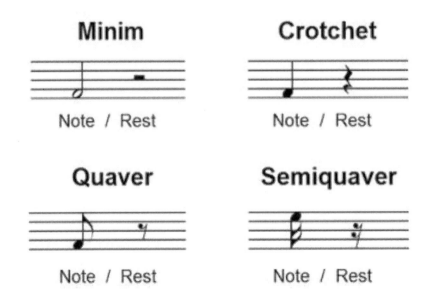

Minim

Note / Rest

Crotchet

Note / Rest

Quaver

Note / Rest

Semiquaver

Note / Rest

Note also that the minim rest looks very similar to the semibreve rest. but there are very subtle differences.

Questions

1. Give the **time name** (e.g. semibreve) of the following rests.

2. Add the correct rest at the places marked with an asterisk

Lesson 1.6 - Tied Notes

Tied notes are **consecutive** notes **of the same pitch** that are joined together by a long smooth line. There can be two or more notes joined together and they are held for the value of the individual notes added together.

Also note the following points:

- Ties can only be between notes that are the **same** pitch. A common mistake is to confuse tied notes with slurred / legato notes which also use the symbol of a curved line. However, a slur or legato symbol is between notes of a **different** pitch

A Slur

- The curved "tie line" is written on the opposite side of the note to the stem. i.e. stems up - ties below.
- If you want to tie more than two notes, you will need more than one tie.

Questions

1. How many crotchets are these tied notes worth?

5

2. How many quavers are these tied notes worth?

9

3. Tie together all **possible** notes in this passage.

4. Finally, next to each of the ties you have drawn above, state the number of beats the combined tied notes add up to.

Lesson 1.7 - Dotted Notes

Dotted notes, (notes with a dot after them) are worth one and a half times the value of the note without the dot. For example, a minim is worth 2 beats, a **dotted minim** is worth "**two plus half of two**" beats = 3 beats.

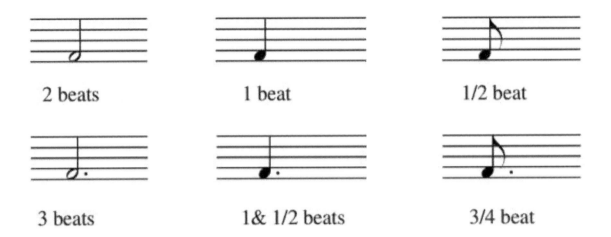

2 beats	1 beat	1/2 beat
3 beats	1& 1/2 beats	3/4 beat

Notice that when a dotted note is on a line of the stave (not like the ones in spaces above) the dot is placed slightly above the line so that it can be seen.

Questions

Write **one** note at the end of each of the following bars, at the place marked with an asterisk, to make the correct number of beats in each bar. (Every bar is in 4/4 time, as in the time signature at the beginning.)

Lesson 1.8 - Accidentals

There are three types of accidental:

- Sharps: These raise the note by a semitone (i.e. you play the very next note to the right whether it is black or white).
- Flats: These lower the note by a semitone.
- Naturals: These cancel the effect of a sharp or a flat.

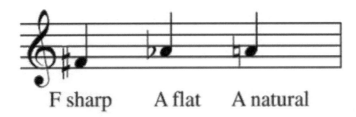

F sharp   A flat   A natural

Notice how these signs are placed directly in front of the note head and notice their size too usually about the same as a space on the stave.

The "horizontal" lines of the sharp and natural are not exactly horizontal, but slightly slanted, so that they can be distinguished from the stave lines.

Notice too how these accidentals are drawn for notes on the lines of the stave.

You also need to remember that the effect of an accidental lasts for the whole bar.

Consider the notes marked 1 to 7 in the stave above.

1) This is a B flat from the key signature.
2) This is also B flat.
3) The accidental makes this a B natural.
4) Because of the previous natural, this B is also, natural.
5) The accidental makes this F sharp.
6) This F is also sharp because of the earlier F sharp.
7) To have a normal F a natural sign is needed to cancel the previous sharp.

Questions

1. Name the following notes in treble clef.

D♯   E♭   A   D♯ C♯   B♭ B   C

2. Name the following notes in bass clef.

B♭   A♯   E   D♯   F G♭ G

3. Add a sharp *in front* of each of these notes.

4. Add a flat *in front* of each of these notes.

5. Cancel the effect of each accidental by placing a natural sign on the next note in that bar, that is on the **same** line or space as the note with the accidental.

Lesson 1.9 - Major Scales

In Grade 1 ABRSM Theory, there are only four keys / scales that you need to know: C, G, D and F major. In Grade 1 Trinity Theory you will not need D major, but it is included in this lesson to cover all basses.

The "Key Signature" is the sharps or flats that appear in that key / scale and these are written at the beginning of the stave just after the clef sign.

Below is the scale of C major, which has **no key signature**.

Notice the letter S written between two pairs of notes in the above scale. These mark the "semitones" which are always between the 3rd/4th and the 7th/8th notes of any major scale as you go up. A semitone is the **smallest interval or gap possible between any two notes on a piano keyboard.**

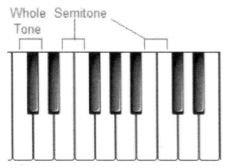

So for example, the notes E and F have no black note between them, therefore, they are a semitone apart, as are B and C. On the other hand C to D is not a semitone, because there is a black note between them - C sharp. (This is actually called a whole tone, but you don't need this for a grade 1 theory exam.)

Notice too that there are no sharps or flats in the scale of C major so no key signature appears next to the clef sign.

The same is not true for G major:

In order to keep the semitones between the 3rd/4th and 7th/8th notes an F sharp needed to be added, because the note immediately below G, is F sharp. Normally this F sharp is written as a key signature next to the clef sign.

Notice also how the key signature looks in the bass clef. In both cases the key signature comes after the clef, but before the time signature. It must also be remembered which line or space the key signature is written on. For example, there is an F on the top line as well as the bottom space of the treble clef. However a key signature of F sharp ALWAYS uses the top line.

Using the same rule, that semitones occur between the 3rd/4th and 7th/8th notes, the scale of D major would have an F sharp and a C sharp.

...and the key signature would look like this.

Notice here how the F sharp is written just before the C sharp.

Questions

1. Name the key of each of these scales. Also write a letter "*s*" between any pairs of notes that make a semitone.

Key .... D maj ....

Key .... G maj ....

Key .... F maj ....

2. Name the key shown by each of these key signatures.

G maj

C maj

D maj

D maj

F maj

C maj

Lesson 1.10 - Degrees of the scale and intervals.

The degree of the scale is very simply the number of the note counting up from the 1st note. So in G major for example the degrees of the scale are as shown below.

1st   2nd   3rd   4th   5th   6th   7th   8th

Intervals are just as easy. An interval is the gap / distance between two notes. There are two kinds of interval.

- Harmonic intervals : The interval between 2 notes that are played at the same time.
- Melodic intervals: The interval between 2 notes played one after the other.

In the scale of G major again the interval between G and B is a "third". Notice we use the word "third" rather than just the number "three".

Harmonic Intervals

2nd   3rd   4th   5th   6th   7th   8th or Octave
(abbreviated to 8ve)

Melodic Intervals

3rd   4th   6th   8ve

Questions

1. **Above** each of the following notes, write a **higher** note, to make the named **harmonic** interval.

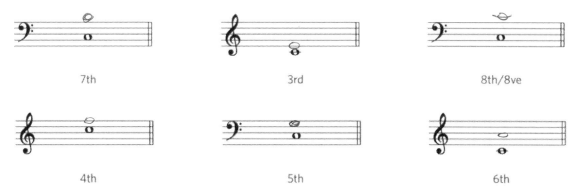

2. Name the degree of the scale of each of the notes marked with an asterisk * (The key is C major).

3. **After** each note write a **higher** note to make the named **melodic** interval.

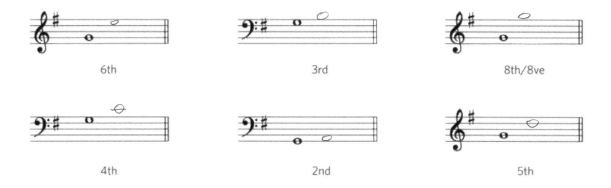

Lesson 1.11 - The Tonic Triad

Another name for the first degree of a scale is called, "The Tonic".

A triad is a group of three notes played at the same time (a chord) and the tonic triad uses the 1st, 3rd and 5th notes of the scale.

In the example below the key signature is G major and the tonic is therefore the note G. The tonic triad consists of the notes G, B and D (the 1st, 3rd and 5th degrees of the scale of G major.

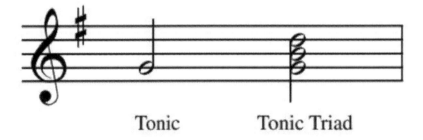

Tonic   Tonic Triad

Questions

1. Name the key of each of these tonic triads

    C maj   D maj   C maj

    F maj   G maj   F maj

2. Write a tonic triad for each of these major key signatures

Lesson 1.12 - Terms and Signs

Below is a table of terms and signs which are needed for a Grade 1 Theory Exam. To test yourself on these, try our FREE flashcards web app on:

https://www.music-online.org.uk/p/lesson-112-theory-quiz-01.html

TERMS

accelerando / accel.	gradually getting quicker
adagio	slow
allegretto	fairly quick (but not as quick as *allegro*)
allegro	quick
andante	at a medium (walking) speed
cantabile	in a singing style
crescendo / cresc. /	gradually getting louder
da capo / D.C.	repeat from the beginning
dal segno / D.S.	repeat from the sign 𝄋
decrescendo / decresc.	gradually getting quieter
diminuendo / dim. /	gradually getting quieter
fine	the end
f / forte	loud
ff / fortissimo	very loud
legato	smoothly
lento	slow
mezzo	half
mf / mezzo forte	moderately loud
mp / mezzo piano	moderately quiet
moderato	moderately
p / piano	quiet
pp / pianissimo	very quiet
poco	a little
rallentando / rall.	gradually getting slower
ritardando / rit.	gradually getting slower
ritenuto / rit.	held back
staccato / stacc.	detached
tempo	speed, time (*a tempo*: in time)
8va	octave

SIGNS

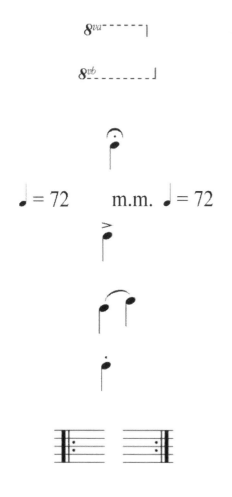

play an octave higher
NB *va* may be omitted
play an octave lower
NB *vb* may be omitted or even
replaced with *va*
pause on the note

72 crochet beats in a minute

accent (placed over or under a
note)

slur (joining two different notes)

dot over / under note = **staccato**

repeat marks – at the second sign
go back to the first sign and
repeat the music from there (if the
first sign is missed out, repeat
from the beginning)

Lesson 2.1 - Ledger Lines

In Grade 2, the notes will go higher and lower than in Grade 1. This is done by the use of ledger lines, small extra lines that are written above or below the stave.

When writing ledger lines it is important to note the following;

The lines should be straight, not sloping up or down as shown by these **"bad"** examples

The lines should be the same distance apart as the stave lines. Below, the first example is too far away, the second , too close.

Each new note needs its own ledger line. Don't join strings of ledger lines together - it will just look like a stave of 6 lines (as below) and that would be confusing.

To work out the names of notes on ledger lines, simply count on or back from the last note just above or just below the stave. Here are some examples of the notes you might come across on ledger lines in Grade 2.

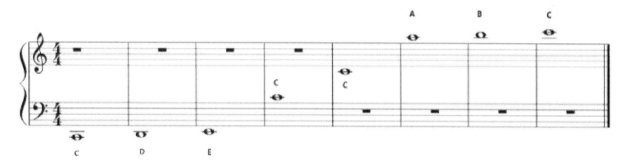

Questions

1. Name the following notes in treble clef.

C   A   G   B   B   C

2. Name the following notes in bass clef

D   D   C   E   E   F

3. Write in the empty bars a note that is one octave *higher* than the previous note.

4. Write in the empty bars a note that is one octave *lower* than the previous note.

Lesson 2.2 - More Time Signatures

In Grade 1 you learned all the time signatures with a number 4 at the bottom. This 4 at the bottom meant that there was a crotchet beat. So "3/4" time was "three crotchet beats in a bar".

3 crotchets in a bar   3 quavers in a bar   3 minims in a bar

In Grade 2 you will come across the numbers 2 and 8 at the bottom of the time signatures.

- An 8 at the bottom means a quaver beat.
- A 2 at the bottom means a minim beat.

Therefore 3/8 time means "three quaver beats in a bar" and 3/2 time means "three minim beats in a bar".

There is also one more sign you should be aware of. A "C"with a line through it is called "cut time" and is an abbreviation for 2/2 time (2 minims in a bar).

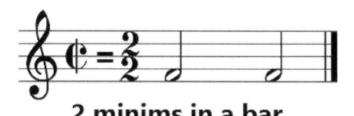

2 minims in a bar

Questions

1. What is the full meaning of these time signatures
a) 3/4 time?   3 c in a b
b) 2/2 time?   2 m i a b
c) 3/8 time?   3 q i a b

2. Add time signatures to each of the following rhythms.

3. Add bar lines to each of the following rhythms.

Lesson 2.3 - More Major Keys

In Grade 1, you learned the major keys of C, G, D and F major. In this lesson you will learn the keys of A, B flat and E flat major. This will take you up to 3 sharps and three flats as required for the following grades at ABRSM and Trinity College London

- Grade 1 ABRSM C, G, D, F major
- Grade 1 Trinity C, G, F major
- Grade 2 ABRSM adds A, B flat and E flat major
- Grade 3 Trinity D, B flat major
- Grade 4 Trinity A, E flat major

Below are shown the key signatures of all the keys you need to know by now along with the tonic triad for each key.

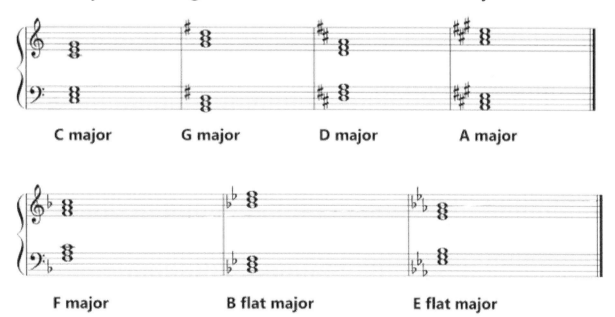

Notice the order and position of the sharps and flats in each key signature. This must be kept the same every time you write these.

A little trick...
You really need to remember the order and position of the one with the most sharps/flats because the ones with less sharps/flats will use the first one or two of these. For example:

A major has three sharps,
D major uses the first two of these three (and in the same order) and
G major uses just the first of these three.

Questions

1. Name the keys of these tonic triads

D major   F major   E♭ major

2. Add the correct clef *and* key signature to each of these tonic triads

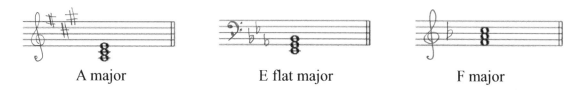

A major   E flat major   F major

3. Write in semibreves, the scale of A major, ascending, with a key signature

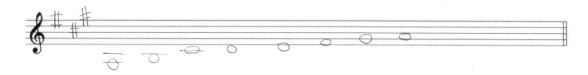

4. Add the correct clef and any necessary sharp or flat signs to make the scale of E flat major. Do **_not_** use a key signature

Lesson 2.4 - Triplets
As required for Grade 2 ABRSM Theory
and Grade 3 Trinity Theory

Triplets simply means three notes played in the time of two. They are usually shown with a small three and a bracket placed above or below (depending on the direction of the note stem), the notes that are to be played as a triplet.

A triplet can be used when two notes that would add up to three of something are used. For example a crotchet and a quaver are worth three quavers. So in this example, the triplet is played in the same time as two normal quavers. (Three triplet quavers = Two normal quavers.)

In each of the following pairs of bars the first bar contains a triplet rhythm and the second, a single note that the first group is worth.

Questions

1. In the empty space following each triplet, write a *single* note that is worth the same time value as the notes *in* the triplet.

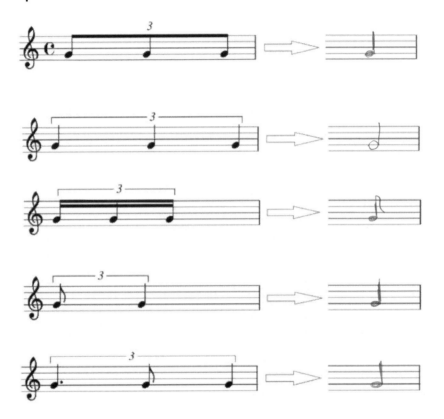

2. Add a time signature to each of these two bars.

Lesson 2.5 - Minor Keys

Minor Keys have key signatures that correspond to those of the major keys. This is shown in the table below.

Key Signature	Major Key	Minor Key
None	C major	A minor
F sharp	G major	E minor
B flat	F major	D minor

In a minor scale however, there are other accidentals and this depends on which form of the minor key you are using. There are three types of minor key that will be used in this course, Natural minors, Harmonic Minors and Melodic Minors.

For Grade 2 ABRSM Theory
you can choose to use either the harmonic minor or melodic minor.

For Grade 2 Trinity Theory
you need to know the natural minor and harmonic minor.

The natural minor is easy, it is simply the notes according to the key signature so D natural minor would look like this.

Key signature of B flat

In a harmonic minor scale the 7th note is raised a semitone in addition to any accidentals you may already have in the key signature.

Therefore:
In A minor there is also a G sharp
In E minor there is also a D sharp
In D minor there is also a C sharp

These raised 7ths do not appear in the key signature but next to the relevant note. So the scale of D *harmonic* minor would look like this.

Key signature of B flat   Raised 7th of C sharp

N.B. Melodic minors will be covered in a later lesson

Questions

1. Name the keys of these tonic triads.

.... A minor .... E minor ....

2. Add the correct clef and key signature to each of these tonic triads.

E minor   D minor

G major   *f maj*

3. Using semibreves, write the key signature and then the scaleof D **harmonic** minor, ascending. Remember to raise the 7th note.

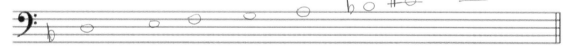

4. Add a clef and any necessary accidentals on the notes themselves *(without writing a key signature),* to make this a scale of E **natural** minor, descending.

Lesson 2.6 - Grouping of Notes

In Lesson 2.2 the new time signatures of 2/2, 3/2, 4/2 and 3/8 were introduced. With these, some new rules about the grouping of notes needs to be observed.

1.When there is a minim beat - basically group quavers together that belong to the same minim beat.   In this example, notice the quavers in the second bar are NOT ALL joined together. Only those that belong to the same minim beat.

(/ = indicates the beats.)

2. Semiquavers should still be grouped just a crotchet's worth at a time. Here, each beamed group of 4 semiquavers make just one crotchet beat, even though all eight are part of the same minim beat.

3. Replace any tied minims by semibreves.

4. In 3/8 time group together all consecutive quavers and semiquavers. It doesn't matter if they are all quavers, all semiquavers or a mixture of both.

Questions

1. Rewrite the following, in notes of **half the value**, starting as shown. Remember to group notes correctly.

2. Rewrite the following, in notes of **twice the value**, starting as shown. Remember to group notes correctly.

3. Rewrite the following, in notes of **half the value**, starting as shown. **Also put in a new time signature** (see Q1 for an example).

Lesson 2.7 - Grouping of Rests.

As with the grouping of notes, rests should usually be grouped,   **_a beat at a time_**.

Look at the following examples for some of the time signatures you should know. (/ = indicates the position of the beats.)

You'll notice that every new beat needs to start with a new rest. For example, in the sixth bar, the two semiquaver rests need to written separately and cannot be combined into a single quaver rest because they belong to different beats.

The only exceptions to the rule are:
a) A whole bar of rest in any of the time signatures covered so far always gets a semibreve rest.

b) The first half or second half of a 4/4 bar (but *not* the two middle beats) can be replaced by a minim rest.

So... these three bars would be **correct**

But this bar would be **incorrect**

Questions

Fill in the gap at the end of each bar with the appropriate rest or rests.

Lesson 2.8 - Terms and Signs

Below is a table of terms and signs which are needed for a Grade 2 Theory Exam. To test yourself on these, try our FREE flashcards web app on:
https://www.music-online.org.uk/p/lesson-28-theory-quiz-02.html

TERMS

al, alla	to the, in the manner of
allargando	broadening
andantino	slightly faster than andante
assai	very
con, col	with
dolce	sweet, soft
e, ed	and
espressivo/express./ espr.	expressive
fp / fortepiano	loud, then immediately soft
giocoso	playful, merry
grave	very slow, solemn
grazioso	graceful
larghetto	rather slow (not as slow as *largo*)
largo	slow, stately
ma	but
maestoso	majestic
meno	less
molto	very, much
mosso, moto	movement
non	not
più	more
presto	fast
senza	without
sf / sfz / sforzando	forced, accented
simile / sim.	in the same way
sostenuto	sustained
tenuto	held
troppo	too much
vivace, vivo	lively, quick

SIGNS

 A wedge indicates super-staccato (*staccatissimo*), played as briefly as possible and possibly accented

 Dots inside a slur over or below the notes mean the notes should be slightly separated (*semi-staccato*),

 marcato means accented

 tenuto means the note is given a slight pressure, and often slightly separated

Lesson 3.1 - Demisemiquavers.

Demisemiquavers are worth half of a semiquaver or in other words, one eighth of a crotchet. They are shown with three beams across the stems.

Notice also how the demisemiquaver rests are written in the third beat.

Demisemiquavers are usually grouped in beats with other notes (e.g. the quaver in the 1st beat above), but some composers will group them, four at a time if there seem to be getting too many in a line and it becomes difficult to see where the beats are.

Questions

1. How many demisemiquavers are worth the same as
a) A quaver   4
b) A dotted crotchet 12
c) A semibreve   32
d) A dotted minim   24

2. Add the missing bar lines to this extract

etc.

3. Add a time signature to this extract.

4. Add a rest or rests at the places marked with an *

Lesson 3.2 - Major Keys with Four Sharps or Flats.

In Level 2 you were expected to know up to 3 sharps or flats, so in this grade there is not that much more to learn. At this stage it might be helpful to look at all the keys you should know in a table.

Key	Key Signature
E major	F♯, C♯, G♯, D♯
A major	F♯, C♯, G♯
D major	F♯, C♯
G major	F♯
C major	No sharps or flats
F major	B♭
B♭ major	B♭, E♭
E♭ major	B♭, E♭, A♭
A♭ major	B♭, E♭, A♭, D♭

Can you see a pattern here?
Each key loses a sharp (or adds a flat as you go down the list)

The order of the sharps / flats is the same and this is the order that they should be written in a key signature as in the example of an E major key signature in the treble clef below.

Notice also that there is an interval of a 5th between each of the keys. This is known as the cycle of 5ths, (because as you learn a few more keys they will go round in a "circle" and start back at the beginning).

For example, from C major, there is an interval of a 5th up to G major, another 5th up to D major, another 5th up to A major etc. etc.

The pattern of 5ths also applies to the order of sharps and flats. From F♯ to C♯ is a 5th, as is C♯ to G♯ - G♯ to D♯ etc etc. Then looking at the flats from D♭ to A♭ is a 5th, likewise A♭ to E♭ and so on. So as long as you can count to five you can work out any key signature.

Questions

1. Write the key signature and tonic triad for each of the following keys.

D major   Bb major   Ab major

2. Add the correct clef and key signature to each of these tonic triads.

A major   E major   Eb major

3. Add the correct clef and any necessary sharp or flatsigns *without key signature* to make this a scale of A major.

4. Write a key signature of 4 sharps and then the major scale of that key, ascending in semibreves in the stave below. Notice the bass clef.

Lesson 3.3 - More Than Two Ledger Lines

In level 2 you learned up to 2 ledger lines in both treble and bass clefs. You will now need to learn three or more lines above or below the stave. Here are some notes on ledger lines that go above the treble clef.

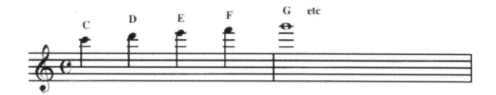

...and here are some that go above and below the stave in the bass clef

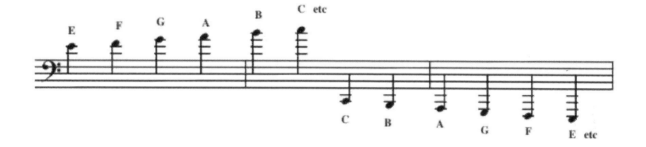

To work out these notes yourself, it is simply a question of counting the steps up or down on the lines or spaces of the ledger lines.

In examinations you may well be asked to write a note in another clef. Be sure to write exactly the same note, not just any note that has the same letter name. The best way to make sure of this is to work out how far the given note is away from middle C (i.e. more than / less than an octave / two octaves above or below)

Questions

1. Name these notes

2. In the following pairs of bars, circle the note in the **second bar,** that is <u>exactly</u> the same as the note in the first bar.

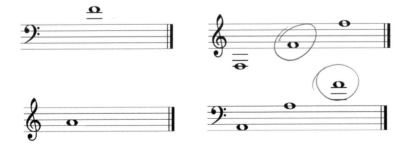

Lesson 3.4 - Transposition

In Grade 3 (ABRSM and Trinity) you will have to transpose (move) a melody up or down an octave from treble to bass clef or vice versa.

For example, the following tune when transposed an octave lower into the bass clef.

...will look like this

The most common mistake in examinations is to write the tune at the wrong octave, often at the same pitch (but in a different clef) or two octaves away. The best way to make sure of getting exactly an octave apart, is to work out how far the given note is away from middle C, as in the previous lesson. In this example the first note is the D *just above middle C* so when transposed down an octave, the first note will be D *just below middle C.*

Another mistake I often see, is that the student starts off OK with the correct note, and then works horizontally, going up or down steps or more, to mirror the intervals in the given original melody. This is fine, but if you miscalculate just one interval on the way, it will mean all the notes following it will also be wrong. If you do use this method, CHECK your last note is still an octave above/below the given note.

Questions

1. In the empty bars below, write a note that is either an octave higher or lower in the other clef.

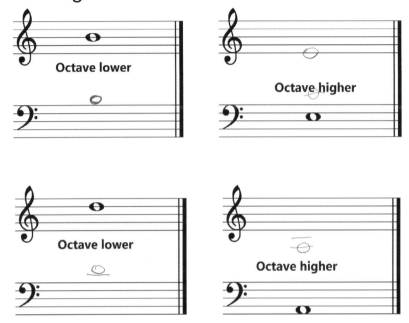

2. Transpose this melody down one octave into the bass clef

3. Transpose this melody up one octave into the treble clef.

Lesson 3.5 - Compound Time

WARNING: This is a long lesson and maybe you might want to make a cup of coffee before starting :)

Up until this point, the only time signatures you came across were in SIMPLE TIME. This means that the beats can be divided in two. e.g. a crotchet can divide into two quavers, a minim can divide into two crotchets etc.

Now you will learn about COMPOUND TIMES where the beats divide into threes. "6/8 time" literally means that there are 6 quavers in a bar, but there are not 6 beats in a bar. Instead there are two dotted crotchet beats in a bar and each dotted crotchet is worth three quavers. Look at these two examples

In the first example notice how the quavers are grouped in threes and the beats in the second bar are dotted crotchets. In the second example there are still six quavers in the bar, but they are grouped in twos, and the beats are crotchets.

The other time signatures you will come across in Grade 3 ABRSM and Trinity are

- 9/8 = Three dotted crotchet beats in a bar
- 12/8 = Four dotted crotchet beats in a bar

There are three more words that you should know,
duple, triple and quadruple.

Their meaning is quite obvious,

- duple time means 2 beats in a bar
- triple time means 3 beats in a bar
- quadruple time means 4 beats in a bar

Examples:

- simple triple time would be 3/4
- compound quadruple would be 12/8

In an exam you may be asked to convert a tune from simple time to compound time, or vice versa. Look at the two examples on the next page

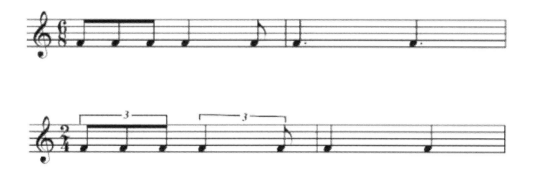

Both of the above rhythms sound exactly the same even though they have different time signatures.
You will notice, to convert:

- from simple to compound - Lose triplets / Add dots
- from compound to simple - Add triplets / Lose dots

Finally, you need to bear in mind, how to group notes and rests together in compound time. The main rule is group things together a beat at a time. Lets consider these four bars

In the first bar, notice how the 4th quaver is not joined to the other three, because it is part of a different beat.

In the second bar, a dotted minim can be used for two beats.

In the third bar there are two separate quaver rests - that is, not joined to make a crotchet rest, because each quaver rest belongs to a different beat.

In the last bar there are separate semiquaver rests. It is true that 2 semiquavers could be replaced by a quaver rest, but composers prefer to finish one quaver at a time i.e. the 1st semiquaver note and semiquaver rest make one quaver, then the next semiquaver rest and note make the next quaver. It is also easier for the performer to read.

One FINAL thing (I know - this was a long one) - just like in 4/4 time where you should only use a minim in the first half or second half but NOT the middle two beats, so also in 12/8 time a dotted minim should not be used for the middle two beats. In the examples below, the first bar is correct, but the 2nd is NOT correct.

Questions

1. Add a time signature to this extract

2. Add bar lines to this extract

3. Add a rest or rests to the places marked with an *

4. Rewrite is 3/4 rhythm in 9/8, keeping the effect the same, the first note has been done for you.

Lesson 3.6 - Minor Keys to 4 sharps or flats.

In **an earlier** you learned all the major keys up to 4 sharps and flats. If you are still unsure about these key signatures, it might be worth revising this lesson before continuing with the minor keys.

Every major key has a corresponding minor key (which is called the relative minor). Therefore the key signatures you learned for the major keys are the same for this lesson.

Key	Key Signature	Relative minor
E major	F♯, C♯, G♯, D♯	C♯ minor
A major	F♯, C♯, G♯	F♯ minor
D major	F♯, C♯	B minor
G major	F♯	E minor
C major	No sharps or flats	A minor
F major	B♭	D minor
B♭ major	B♭, E♭	G minor
E♭ major	B♭, E♭, A♭	C minor
A♭ major	B♭, E♭, A♭, D♭	F minor

♯6

The only thing that is different in these minor keys is that the 7th note in a harmonic minor is raised by a semitone. So for example in D minor the 7th note is normally C. If we raise it by a semitone it becomes C♯.

D minor scale

NOTICE that the C sharp is not part of the key signature. It is written as an extra accidental on the note itself.

Here is a summary of the raised 7ths for all the minor keys up to four sharps or flats.

Minor Key	Raised 7th
C♯ minor	B♯
F♯ minor	E♯
B minor	A♯
E minor	D♯
A minor	G♯
D minor	C♯
G minor	F♯
C minor	B♮
F minor	E♮

Notice especially the last two are naturals, not sharps. This is because the 7th note according to the key signature is a flat, and when you raise it, it becomes a natural. For example the 7th note of C minor according to the key signature is B flat, which becomes a B natural in the harmonic minor.

One final thing to remember is that if you are taking an ABRSM examination you may be asked to say which form of minor scale you have used - which in this case, remember, is the *harmonic minor.*

Questions

1. Name the key of this scale

Key *harmonic* C minor

2. Add a clef and any necessary accidentals to make this a scale of F harmonic minor. Do NOT use a key signature.

F harmonic minor

A♭ maj

B E B C
D E A B F
D E A C
D E A A

3. Write a key signature and tonic triad for these *minor* keys.

C minor

C♯ minor

E maj

E maj

C
G
D
A
E

4. Add the correct clef and key signature to each of these tonic triads.

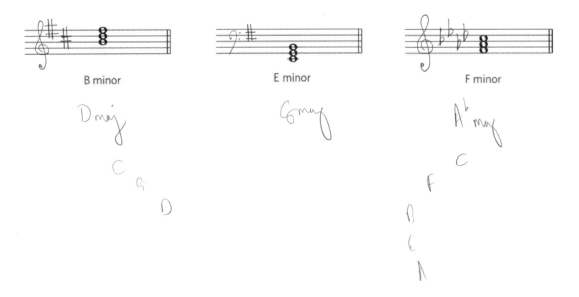

B minor   E minor   F minor

D maj   G maj   A♭ maj

C   C
  G   F
    D   B
             E
             A

Lesson 3.7 - Intervals (Major, Minor and Perfect)

Previously you had to write the interval number between two notes. For example 3rd, 4th, 5th etc. Now you will also have to state what type of 3rd, 4th or 5th the interval is.

First of all consider all the intervals that occur between the tonic as the lower note and all the other notes of a major scale

Major 2nd   Major 3rd   Perfect 4th   Perfect 5th   Major 6th   Major 7th   Perfect Octave

Notice that the 4th, 5th and Octave are called "perfect" - this is because they are the same in major and minor scales.

The only other intervals you need to consider for now are the minor 3rd, minor 6th and minor 7th. Compare these to their major equivalents.

Major 3rd   Minor 3rd   Major 6th   Minor 6th   Major 7th   Minor 7th

It is easy to see from the above that a minor interval is always a semitone smaller than a major interval.

For example -
- C to E is a major third,
- C to E flat is a minor third

So to work out any interval, simply think of the major scale of the lowest note. If the higher note is in that major scale, for 2nds, 3rds, 6ths and 7ths, then the interval is MAJOR. If it is a semitone smaller it is MINOR.

Remember - there is no such thing as a major or minor 4th, 5th or octave. For now, (there will be more advanced intervals explained in higher grades) just describe 4ths, 5ths and Octaves as *Perfect.*

Finally, you might come across the descriptions *harmonic* and *melodic* when referring to intervals. This should cause no difficulties. Harmonic intervals are made by notes that are played together - a chord. Melodic intervals are formed by notes that played one after the other - in a melody.

Harmonic interval of
a major 3rd

Melodic interval of
a major 3rd

Questions

1. Name these intervals by number *and* type.

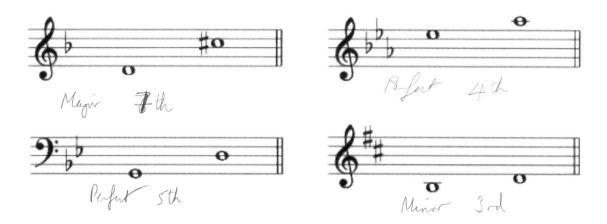

Major 7th

Perfect 4th

Perfect 5th

Minor 3rd

2. Write another note above the following to make the named harmonic intervals.

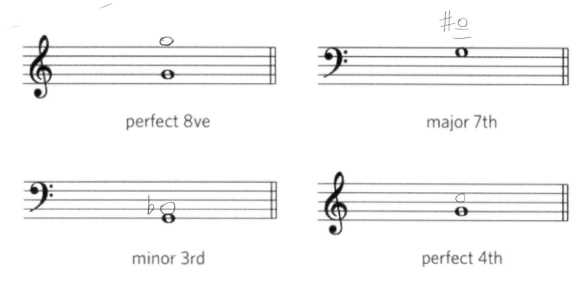

perfect 8ve

major 7th

minor 3rd

perfect 4th

Lesson 3.8 - Simple phrase structure.

In this grade you will be required to mark where phrases begin and end. There are a few simple clues to help you identify where they start and finish.

Look at this example

1st phrase

2nd phrase

2nd phrase continued

- Phrases tend to be the same length (or they probably will be at this simple level), here each phrase is exactly 4 bars.

- Phrases tend to start on the same beat of the bar - i.e. if the 1st phrase starts on an upbeat then so will the 2nd. In this example both phrases start on an upbeat.

- Phrases tend to end on a longer note. Notice here the dotted minim at the end of each phrase.

- Phrases tend to have similar rhythmic patterns to each other. Here both phrases have exactly the same rhythm.

Questions

Both the following extracts have two phrases. Add phrase markings to show *exactly* where each phrase starts and finishes.

1.

2.

Lesson 3.9 - Musical Terms

Below is a table of terms and signs which are needed for a Grade 3 Theory Exam. To test yourself on these, try our FREE flashcards web app on:

https://www.music-online.org.uk/p/lesson-39-theory-quiz-03.html

adagietto	rather slow (faster than *adagio*)
ad libitum, ad lib.	at choice, to be played freely
agitato	agitated
alla breve	with a minim beat, equivalent to 2/2,
amore	love (*amoroso* – loving)
anima	soul, spirit
animato	animated, lively
animando	becoming lively
ben	well
brio	vigour
comodo	convenient, comfortable
deciso	with determination
delicato	delicate
energico	energetic
forza	force
largamente	broadly
leggiero	light, nimble
marcato / marc.	emphatic, accented
marziale	in a military style
mesto	sad
pesante	heavy
prima / primo	first
risoluto	bold, strong
ritmico	rhythmically
rubato / tempo rubato	with some freedom of time
scherzando / scherzoso	playful, joking
seconda / secondo	second
semplice	simple, plain
sempre	always
stringendo	gradually getting faster
subito	suddenly
tanto	so much
tranquillo	calm
triste / tristamente	sad, sorrowful
volta	time (e.g. *prima volta* – first time)

Lesson 4.1 - Time Signatures - REVIEW

By Grade 4 Music Theory, you need to know all simple and compound time signatures.
To summarize:

For Simple Time Signatures

- Top number tells you how many beats in a bar
- Bottom number tells you the type of beat

  /2 minim beat
  /4 crotchet beat
  /8 quaver beat
  /16 semiquaver beat

Therefore some of the new time signatures you might come across at this level might be

  2/8 - 2 quaver beats in a bar
  4/2 - 4 minim beats in a bar

For Compound Time Signatures

Remember that the beats are grouped into into threes
So for example,
6/4 time, although it contains 6 crotchets in every bar is actually 2 DOTTED MINIM BEATS IN A BAR and the way the notes are grouped will reflect this.
Take a look at this example

The dashes / indicate where the beats are

You will notice that both lines have exactly the same lengths of notes, but in 6/4 time the beats are dotted minims. In 3/2 time, the beats are just minims. The notes need to be grouped together to reflect this.

For example the minim in the first bar needs to be split into two tied crotchets, in 3/2 time, because the two halves belong to different beats.

Similarly, the semibreve at the end must be split into a crotchet tied to a dotted minim in 6/4 time because these two notes belong to two separate beats.

Questions

1. Add a time signature to each of the following bars.

2. Under each bar above, describe the time signature as "simple or compound" **and** as "duple, triple or quadruple.

3. Rewrite the following passage in 3/2 time grouping the notes in minims rather than dotted minims.

Lesson 4.2 - Breves and Double Dotting

Breves

The prefix "semi" on a word means half. Therefore a semibreve is half of a breve and the latter is worth 8 crotchets. This is what a breve and its equivalent rest look like:

NOTE: Up until now you learned that a whole bar of rest was always indicated by a semibreve rest. However for a whole bar of rest in 4/2 time you would need to put a breve rest as shown above.

Double Dotting

You already should know that dotted notes are worth half as much again as the original note. Double dotting is where there is another "half of the half" added on.

For example:

Minim = 2 crotchets

Dotted minim = 2 plus half of 2 = 3 crotchets

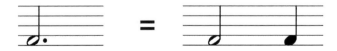

A **_double dotted minim_** =

2 + half of 2 + half of half of 2 = 3 and a half crotchets.

Similarly a double dotted crotchet is worth one and three quarter crotchets and a double dotted quaver is worth seven eighths of a crotchet.

Questions

1. A breve is worth how many
   a) minims
   b) quavers
   c) demisemiquavers?

2. Write the correct rest in each of the places below, marked with an asterisk.

Lesson 4.3 - Duplets

You should already know that triplets are 3 notes played in the space of 2. Duplets are simply 2 notes played in the space of 3 and are shown by placing a bracketed two above the relevant notes.

This would be quite useful if you needed to convert a piece from simple time into compound time.

For example, if you were asked to convert this 4/4 rhythm into compound time

it would become

The duplets in this example occur where two notes are played in the space of where you would normally find three.

Remember in 12/8 time a beat normally contains 3 quavers. If you only have 2 notes in a beat - a duplet sign is needed.

Notice also that the crotchet beats of 4/4, become **_dotted crotchet beats_** in 12/8

Finally note there is no need for the triplet sign used in the 4/4 rhythm because the beat in 12/8 contains 3 quavers anyway.

Questions

1. Write this 3/4 rhythm in 9/8 time so that it sounds the same. The first note has been done for you.

2. Now write this 9/8 rhythm in 3/4 time, again, so that it sounds the same.

3. Now complete this sentence by inserting the words *"duplets", "triplets", "dots".*

"When converting from simple time to compound time we add _____ and _____ and lose _____ "

4. Now write a similar sentence starting, "When converting from compound time to...............

Lesson 4.4 - Alto Clef

The alto clef is between the treble and bass clef and its middle line is middle C. This is what an alto clef and a Middle C written on it, look like

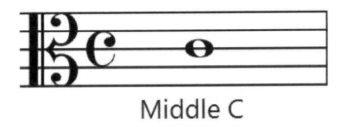

Middle C

Apart from simply naming the notes of the alto clef, an examination may require you to write out a simple melody from treble or bass clef into alto clef or vice versa.

For example - if you had to write this out in treble clef :

it would become this:

You need to be careful that you don't just write the correct letter, but also at the correct octave. Remember that middle C in the alto clef is on the *middle line.*

Questions

1. Name the following notes

2. Rewrite the following passage into alto clef, using the empty stave below

3. Rewrite the following passage into treble clef, using the empty stave below

Lesson 4.5 - Double Sharps and Double Flats

A sharp raises notes by a semitone - a double sharp raises notes by two semitones. Similarly a double flat lowers notes by two semitones. The symbols used are shown below.

You may have already noticed that all notes have more than one name. For example, F sharp = G flat

Similarly **F double sharp = G** and **G double flat = F**

On the piano keyboard, sometimes there is no black note between two white notes and in this case extra care must be taken. So for example, a B double sharp is the same as a C sharp or D flat.

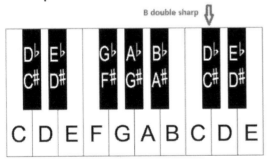

These are called "***enharmonic equivalents***". In fact every note always has two enharmonic equivalents. All the following are in fact the same pitch.

Questions

1. Complete this sentence: "**G double sharp, is an enharmonic equivalent of** _____ **and** _____ .

2. Next two each of these notes, write two more notes that are enharmonic equivalents.

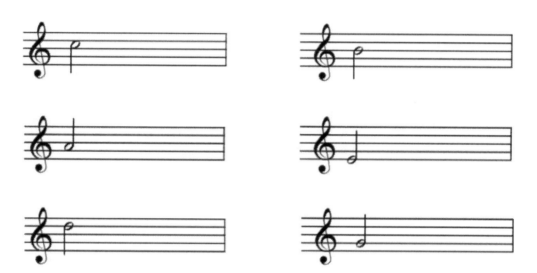

Lesson 4.6 - Keys up to 5 sharps or flats

Major Keys

In level 3 you learned up to 4 sharps or flats, so in this level, there is not that much more to learn. The new scales for this grade are shown in bold in this table.

Key	Key Signature
B major	**F♯, C♯, G♯, D♯, A♯**
E major	F♯, C♯, G♯, D♯
A major	F♯, C♯, G♯
D major	F♯, C♯
G major	F♯
C major	No sharps or flats
F major	B♭
B♭ major	B♭, E♭
E♭ major	B♭, E♭, A♭
A♭ major	B♭, E♭, A♭, D♭
D♭ major	**B♭, E♭, A♭, D♭, G♭**

As was explained in the previous level, there is a pattern of fifths between all these key signatures. Starting at the bottom with D flat major the fifth note of each scale is the scale above in the table. A flat is the fifth note of D flat major, E flat is the fifth note of A flat major etc.

Also the distance between all the sharps and flats is a fifth.
From G flat to D flat is a 5th
From D flat to A flat is a 5th

The same is true with the sharps
From F sharp to C sharp is a 5th
From C sharp to G sharp is a 5th

Here is how these key signatures look in the bass and treble clef

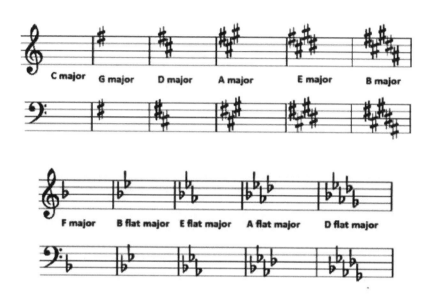

Notice also the pattern of the placement, where you put the sharps or flats. There is a pattern with the sharps that goes high, low, high, low, but the final A sharp breaks the pattern. With the flats it is easier, start low and then alternate high, low, high, low.

Minor Keys

You previously learned that every major key has a relative minor. Therefore the two new major keys you just learned will have two new relative minors. i.e.

G♯ minor is the relative minor of B major ...and
B♭ minor is the relative minor of D♭ major.

But there's more!!

Up until now in this course you have only needed to know the harmonic form of the minor scale with its raised 7th. In Grade 4 ABRSM and Grade 3 Trinity College Music Theory, you also need to know the melodic minor scale.

In a melodic minor scale the 6th and 7th notes are raised on the way up **ONLY** and these notes revert back to the key signature on the way down.

Consider this scale of G minor

Raised
6th + 7th

6th +7th as
Key Sig.

On the way up the 6th and 7th notes which are normally E flat and F, (according to the Key Signature), are raised to E natural and F sharp and on the way down they revert back to F and E flat (as per Key Signature).

This table summarizes all the key signatures of the minor scales you need for this level along with the notes that need to be raised for both harmonic and melodic minor scales.

Key	Key Signature	Harmonic Raise 7th	Melodic Raise 6th & 7th Ascending only
G♯ minor	F♯, C♯, G♯, D♯, A♯	Fx	E♯ & Fx
C♯ minor	F♯, C♯, G♯, D♯	B♯	A♯ & B♯
F♯ minor	F♯, C♯, G♯	E♯	D♯ & E♯
B minor	F♯, C♯	A♯	G♯ & A♯
E minor	F♯	D♯	C♯ & D♯
A minor	No sharps or flats	G♯	F♯ & G♯
D minor	B♭	C♯	B♮ & C♯
G minor	B♭, E♭	F♯	E♮ & F♯
C minor	B♭, E♭, A♭	B♮	A♮ & B♮
F minor	B♭, E♭, A♭, D♭	E♮	D♮ & E♮
B♭ minor	B♭, E♭, A♭, D♭, G♭	A♮	G♮ & A♮

Notice the F double sharp in G♯ minor as you raise the 7th - F♯ to Fx

Questions

1. Name the major key that corresponds to the following key signatures.

2. Write a key signature of D flat major, taking care of the order and placement of the accidentals.

3. Write the following scales **with key signatures** remembering to add **any extra accidentals** that are **not in the key signature.**

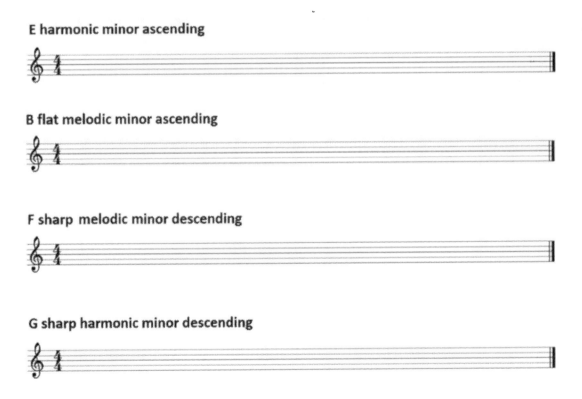

Lesson 4.7 - Technical Names for Degrees of the Scale

This requirement is simply a question of learning seven words corresponding to the seven degrees of the scale - and you already know the first one!

In Trinity College Theory they are introduced one or two at a time from Grades 1-6 whereas in ABRSM Music Theory, they are all introduced together at Grade 4.

1st degree of the scale = tonic
2nd degree of the scale = supertonic
3rd degree of the scale = mediant
4th degree of the scale = subdominant
5th degree of the scale = dominant
6th degree of the scale = submediant
7th degree of the scale = leading note
8th degree of the scale = tonic (same as 1st)

There is a pattern to observe that might help you remember some of these. The prefix "sub" means below. So if the dominant is the 5th note *up* from the tonic, then the *sub*dominant is the 5th note *down* from the tonic. The same is true for mediant (3rd note up) and submediant (3rd note down)

... and that's about it. Take a moment to try to memorise these seven terms and then try the questions on the next page.

Questions

1. Given that the first note in each of the bars below is the **key note,** state the technical name for the second note in each bar.

2. In the key of D flat major, write the following notes

Tonic   Submediant   Supertonic

Lesson 4.8 - Writing Chromatic Scales

A chromatic scale is one where every semitone between two given notes is played. When writing a chromatic scale it will mean that you will have to use some letters more than once e.g. a G followed by a G sharp. Generally try to avoid using a particular letter more than twice. i.e. don't write G flat, G, G sharp.

When writing a chromatic scale there will be more than one possible correct answer.

the example shown here could also be written like this

Both these are exactly the same notes, written in two different ways. Notice also the F sharp key signature. You may have to do an exercise with or without a key signature in an examination.

Questions

1. Turn the following into chromatic scales by adding accidentals.

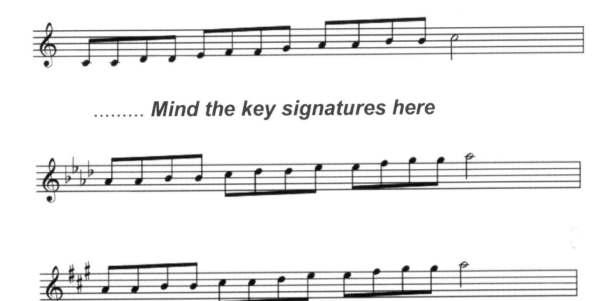

.... *Mind the key signatures here*

2. Write a chromatic scale, starting on the given note, one octave ascending.

NOTE - there is more than one possible correct answer to this question.

Lesson 4.9 - Intervals (Augmented and Diminished)

In level 3, you learned the prefixes major, minor and perfect as applied to intervals. To summarize; 4ths, 5ths and octaves are perfect. 2nds, 3rds, 6ths and 7ths are major if they occur in the major scale of the lower note.

Major 2nd   Major 3rd   Perfect 4th   Perfect 5th   Major 6th   Major 7th   Perfect Octave

Minor intervals are a semitone less than major intervals.

Major 3rd   Minor 3rd   Major 6th   Minor 6th   Major 7th   Minor 7th

In this lesson there are two *more* prefixes as applied to intervals: **Augmented and Diminished.**

- Perfect and major intervals can be augmented (increased by a semitone)

- Perfect and minor intervals can be diminished (decreased by a semitone).

Let's consider some examples

- F to A is a *major* 3rd (A is the 3rd note of F major)
- F to A sharp is an *augmented* 3rd (increased by a semitone)
- F to A flat is a *minor* 3rd (decreased by a semitone)
- F to A double flat is a *diminished* 3rd (a minor 3rd decreased by yet another semitone).

- F to B flat is a *perfect* 4th (B flat is the 4th note of F major and remember there is no such thing as a major or minor 4th)
- F to B natural is an *augmented* 4th. (Increased by a semitone).
- F to B double flat is a *diminished* 4th (Decreased by a semitone).

Many people find this quite complicated but if you follow this flow chart you can't go wrong.

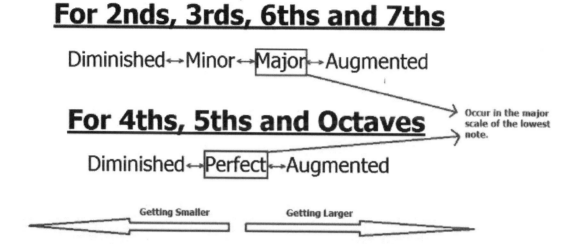

For 2nds, 3rds, 6ths & 7ths

- If the upper note is in the major scale of the lower note it is MAJOR
- If it is a semitone less it is MINOR
- If it is a semitone more it is AUGMENTED
- If it is 2 semitones less it is DIMINSHED

For 4ths, 5ths and Octaves.

- If the upper note is in the major scale of the lower note it is PERFECT.
- If it is a semitone less it is DIMINISHED
- If it is a semitone more it is AUGMENTED.

The only problem may arise if the lower note is one you do not know the major scale of, C sharp to A flat for example.

If you asked the interval between C sharp and A flat first consider the major scale of a note you do know i.e. C major.

Now C - A is a major 6th

A is the 6th note of C major
So C - A is a major 6th

...so C# to A is a semitone less i.e. a minor 6th

C sharp - A is one semitone
smaller than C - A so this is a
minor 6th

and C# to Ab would be a diminished 6th

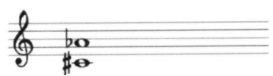

A flat is yet another semitone closer to
C sharp than A, so this interval is a
diminished 6th

Questions

Name the interval between the two notes in each bar

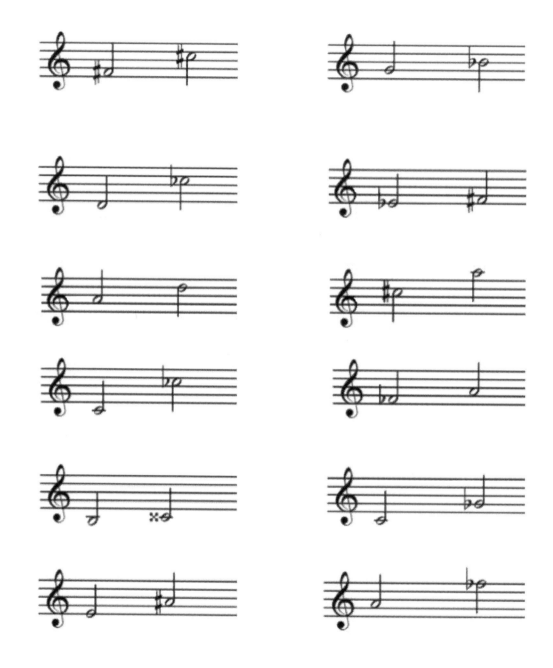

Lesson 4.10 - Writing and Recognizing Chords

The chords you will need to know for Grade 4 ABRSM Music Theory, are those built on the Tonic, the Subdominant and the Dominant. You will remember these are the 1st, 4th and 5th degrees of the scale.

Trinity College introduces the Dominant chord in Grade 3 and the Subdominant in Grade 4.

Previously you have come across the Tonic Triad where a chord was built on the key note - the "tonic" using the 1st, 3rd and 5th degrees of the scale. The principle is the same for the two new chords, but you just need to build the chord starting on the 4th or 5th degree of the scale. Here are the three triads in the key of E major.

Tonic Triad

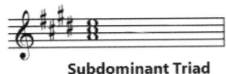

Subdominant Triad

Dominant Triad

There are two other things to bear in mind in this topic:

1. In a minor key the dominant triad contains the 7th degree of the scale and you will remember that the 7th note of a harmonic minor is raised. So for example in the scale of E *minor* - the 7th note is raised to D sharp. This 7th degree of the scale occurs in the dominant triad and so the dominant triad contains a D sharp. In fact the middle note of the dominant triad in any minor key is raised.

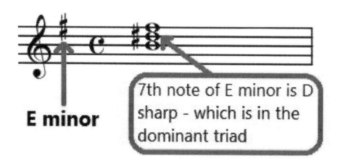

E minor

7th note of E minor is D sharp - which is in the dominant triad

2. Triads may be written in "open position" which means that all the notes might not necessarily be close to each other. They may even cover two clefs. The trick to easily recognizing the chord, is to look at the bass note. Both the chords here, for example are a tonic triad of C major.

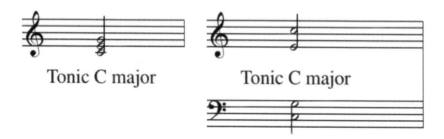

Tonic C major   Tonic C major

Questions

1. Name these chords in "*open position*".
The Key is D flat major

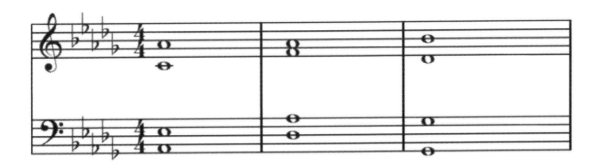

2. Write the chords asked for in *"closed position"*.
The Key is F sharp minor.

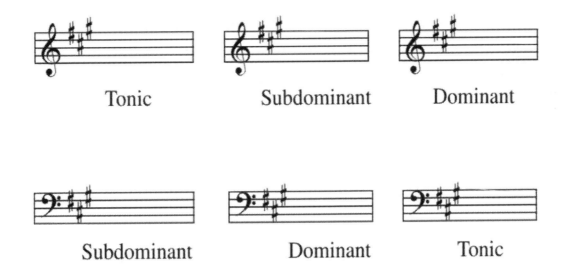

Lesson 4.11 - Ornaments

There are 6 types of ornament you need to know for Grade 4 ABRSM / Grade 5 Trinity   Music Theory.

An ornament is a note or group of notes that "decorate" the main melody note. You will only need to know the names of the signs at this stage and will **NOT** be required to write out how the ornament sounds.

Trill

A trill is a rapid alternation between the written note and the note above it. Sometimes there may be a small turn at the end, don't let this put you off. Also depending on the period of music the starting note may be the written note **or** the upper note.

Turn

There are two kinds of turn you need to know. The first is the turn **on** a note where you start on the upper note, then a rapid triplet descending down through the main note to the lower note and returning to the main note.

The second type is a turn **between** notes. In this case you start with the written note, before doing the rapid triplet as above

Mordents

Again there are two types, the upper and lower mordent, they both start on the main written note and rapidly move one step away and back again, the only difference between the two being, the upper mordent steps up and the lower mordent steps down. Notice the slash in the sign for a lower mordent.

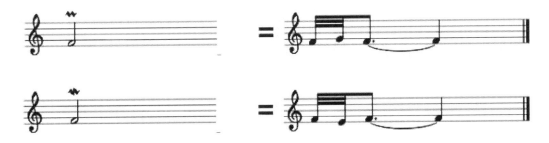

Acciaccatura

This is often called a **grace note** and may be called such in an exam. It is also sometimes referred to as a crush note describing its effect of rapidly crushing the smaller note just before and onto the main written note. However, this term is best avoided in the exam, even if it is helpful in remembering its function.

Appoggiatura

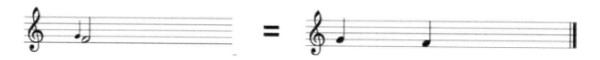

The effect of an Appoggiatura is very similar to that of the acciaccatura, except is is slower, often dividing the time value of the main written note in half. Notice the sign for the appoggiatura, does **not** have the "slash" through it like the grace note.

Questions

1. Name the following ornaments.

2. Name the following ornaments written out in full.

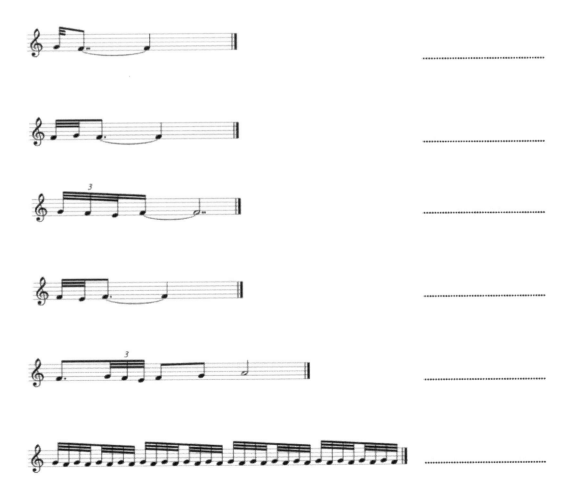

Lesson 4.12 - Orchestral Instruments

Some basic questions about the instruments of the orchestra will be asked at examination for Grade 4 ABRSM Music Theory. In Trinity College Music Theory exams, this knowledge starts at Grade 3 but only for a limited number of instruments, namely violin, cello, flute and bassoon.

Questions might include:
- the names of the different instruments and to which orchestral family they belong.
- the range of these instruments and a knowledge of which clefs are used by them.
- some terms and signs that apply specifically to certain instruments

Instrument families (arranged in pitch order high-low)
- **Strings:**
Violin, Viola, Cello, Double Bass
- **Woodwind:**
Flute, Oboe, Clarinet, Bassoon
- **Brass:**
Trumpet, Horn, Trombone, Tuba
- **Percussion:**
Timpani, Xylophone, Drums (various kinds) Cymbals etc.

One common questions with regard to percussion instruments is to differentiate between tuned (those that possess a specific pitch or pitches e.g. timpani) and untuned (those that have no specific pitch e.g. bass drum). The above lists are by no means exhaustive but do list some of the more popular instruments

Clefs

The majority of instruments use the treble clef most of the time with the exceptions of the following -

Alto Clef - Viola

Tenor Clef - Tenor Trombone

Bass Clef - Cello, Double Bass, Bassoon, Bass Trombone and Tuba

Other instruments may use other clefs sometimes, but the ones given above are the most commonly used.

Instrument Specific Terms and Signs

Sordini (or sord) - Mutes as used by stringed and brass instruments.

The following signs are used just by string instruments.

1. Down bow
2. Up bow
3. Play the notes within the slur with one bow
4. Short for pizzicato meaning plucked
5. On the G string
6. Play near the bridge

The final set of terms and signs are more specifically for the piano.

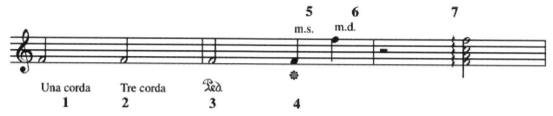

1. Una corda stands for 'one string'* which is to use the left pedal (damper pedal) on the piano

2. Tre corda or 'three strings' means to lift the left (damper) pedal.

3. Ped is short for 'pedal' meaning use the right or sustain pedal.

4. Release the right (sustain) pedal.

5. m.s. - mano sinistra i.e. play with the left hand.

6. m.d. - mano destra i.e. play with the right hand.

7. Spread the notes of a chord, starting at the bottom much like a rapid arpeggio.

*The term Una Corda comes from the fact that traditionally on a piano the sound is made quieter by moving the hammer that hit the strings to one side so that it only strikes one of three strings.

Questions

1. Name a brass instrument that uses the bass clef.

2. What does the abbreviation *pizz.* mean?

3. What instrument is most likely to play the passage below?

4. What clues in the passage led you to your answer for Question 3?

Lesson 4.13 - Musical Terms

Below is a table of terms and signs which are needed for a Grade 4 Theory Exam. Note that in ABRSM you will need to know some **French Terms** as well as Italian ones. To test yourself on these, try our FREE flashcards web app on: https://www.music-online.org.uk/p/lesson-413-theory-quiz-0.html

Italian Terms

affettuoso	tenderly
affrettando	hurrying
amabile	amiable, pleasant
appassionato	with passion
calando	getting softer, dying away
cantando	singing
come	as, similar to
facile	easy
fuoco	fire
giusto	proper, exact
l'istesso	the same
morendo	dying away
niente	nothing
nobilmente	nobly
perdendosi	dying away
possibile	possible
quasi	as if, resembling
sonoro	resonant, with rich tone
sopra	above
sotto	below
veloce	swift
voce	voice

French Terms

à	to, at
animé	animated, lively
assez	enough, sufficient
avec	with
cédez	yield, relax with speed
douce	sweet
en dehors	prominent
et	and
légèrement	light
lent	slow
mais	but
moins	less
modéré	at a moderate speed
non	not
peu	little
plus	more
presser	hurry
ralentir	slow down
retenu	held back
sans	without
très	very
un / une	one
vif	lively
vite	quick

Lesson 5.1 - Irregular Time Signatures

The only new time signatures in this lesson are

- 5/8 - 5 Quavers in a bar
- 7/8 - 7 Quavers in a bar
- 5/4 - 5 Crotchets in a bar
- 7/4 - 7 Crotchets in a bar

They are all introduced at Grade 5 ABRSM music theory and the first three at Grade 4 Trinity College music theory.

You will remember that the top number tells you how many beats are in a bar and the bottom number tells you the type of beat. So for example 5/8 time would be 5 quaver beats in a bar.

Examination questions typically require you to

- either add bar lines to a short passage of music, where the time signature is already given,
- or add time signatures where the bar lines are already given.

Otherwise, there is nothing more complicated than that - **It is just a matter of counting.**

Questions

1. Add a time signature to each of the following bars.

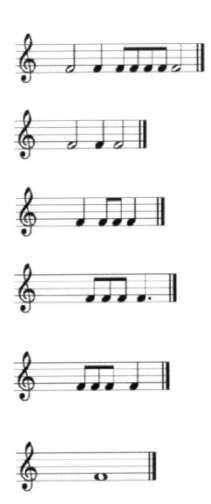

2. Add bar lines to the following extract in 5/8 time

Lesson 5.2 - The Tenor Clef

The tenor clef is just below the alto clef and its 4th line is middle C.

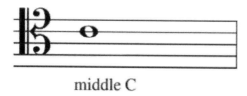

middle C

Apart from simply naming the notes of the tenor clef, an examination may require you to write out a simple melody from treble or bass clef into tenor clef or vice versa.

For example;

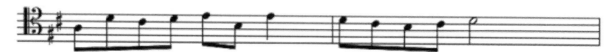

...becomes:

The most common mistake made in examinations is to write the correct letter name but at the wrong octave, so for reference, compare the notes you have written to how far away from middle C they are.

The other thing to notice carefully here is the position of the sharps. For all the other clefs; treble, bass and alto the sharps start off with a "higher-lower-higher-lower" pattern but for the tenor clef it starts with the first sharp in a lower position. For the flat key signatures there is no such distinction. All the clefs will start with a flat in a lower position.

 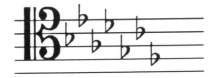

Questions

1. Name the following Tenor Clef Notes.

2. Rewrite the following Treble Clef melody in Tenor Clef, so that it sounds the same.

3. Write a tenor clef followed by a key signature of A major.

Lesson 5.3 - Transposition

Up until now you have only had to transpose a melody up or down an octave. There are many Orchestral Instruments which are called transposing instruments. This means that they play things at a different pitch to what they read.
For example, a French Horn would read the note "E" but be playing an "A" in what we call concert pitch. This all sounds a bit complicated and daunting but if you follow a few simple rules it is not that bad.

a) Firstly you will be told in the exam how far to transpose the melody for a given transposing instrument (you don't have to work that bit out yourself), for example up a perfect fifth or down a minor third.

b) Next you need to transpose your key signature. If you were told to transpose everything down a minor 3rd and you were given a key signature of A flat major, you write the key signature a minor third down from A flat, that is F major.

c) Then simply write each note an interval of a third lower than what you are given. You don't really have to worry about the "*minor*" bit of minor 3rd, because the key signature should take care of that.

d) Where there are accidentals - if the given note has been raised or lowered then you need to do the same to the transposed note.

Consider this example:

Applying points a) - d) above:

a. You are told to transpose down a perfect 5th

b. Transpose the key signature (in this case C major) down a 5th to become F major

c. Write each note a 5th lower

d. Account for any accidentals, so for example, the F sharp in the 3rd bar has been raised from the original, so you need to **raise** the corresponding note in the transposed version. In this case a B flat is raised to a B natural.

Sometimes you might be asked to transpose *without* a key signature. In this case

....pretend you're in C major

....work out your new transposed key

.... instead of using a key signature just keep the accidentals of your new transposed key in your mind. In the above example it will be C major so that will be easy.

This is how the answer will look for the above question, if it had asked you to transpose *without* a key signature.

Notice no need for a B natural
here as there is no key signature

Most questions will require you however to change and use a key signature.

Questions

1. Transpose this melody down a major 2nd. The new key signature has been done for you.

2. Transpose this melody up a minor 3rd **with a new key signature.**

3. Transpose this melody down a perfect 5th **without a key signature.**

Lesson 5.4 - The Cycle of Fifths

In Level 4 you were expected to know up to 5 sharps or flats, so in this grade there is not that much more to learn. The new scales needed at Grade 5 Theory are highlighted in yellow in this chart.

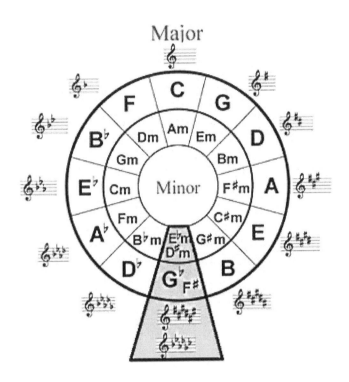

You should notice that there is a pattern of fifths between all these key signatures. Starting at C major, the distance between each scale going round clockwise is a 5th. From C-G is a 5th, from G-D is a 5th etc. Etc.

Also the distance between all the sharps and flats is a fifth.

From G flat to D flat is a 5th
From D flat to A flat is a 5th

The same is true with the sharps

From F sharp to C sharp is a 5th
From C sharp to G sharp is a 5th

Here you can see the positions of the sharps as needed for each clef.

Notice that there is a nice pattern for the flats of **"down-up-down-up-down-up"** for **all** the clefs. Unfortunately with the sharp key signatures, it is not so uniform. For three of the clefs (treble, bass and alto) it starts off with a nice pattern of "up-down-up-down" but then it goes down again and finally up. Additionally, you will notice that the tenor clef is the complete opposite with the pattern of the sharps going **"down-up-down-up-down-up"**

Remember that in an examination, the position of the sharps **is** important.

Questions

1. Name the major **and** minor keys that correspond to each of these key signatures.

2. Write a scale of E flat **melodic** minor ascending, using a key signature.

Lesson 5.5 - Irregular time divisions

Previous lessons have dealt with triplets and duplets. Now you will learn how beats are divided into 5, 6, 7 or 9. Groups of 5, 6 or 7, known as **quintuplets, sextuplets and septuplets** respectively, are equal to 4 of the same type of note value. For example 5 'quintuplet' quavers are worth the same as 4 normal quavers, or in other words a minim.

Groups of 9 are equal to 8 of the same type of note value.

Consider these examples:

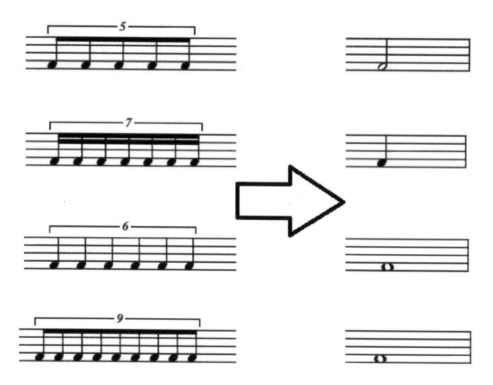

In each of these examples the group of notes on the left is worth the same time value as the single note on the right.

Questions

In each of the empty bars on the right, write a **_single note_** equal to the tuplets on the left.

Lesson 5.6 - Intervals Greater than an Octave

All the intervals you have studied up until now have been an octave or less. In this lesson, suitable for Grade 5 ABRSM and Grade 4 Trinity college, you will learn how to name intervals of more than an octave. This is actually very easy as an octave plus a perfect 5th becomes a "compound perfect fifth".

Some musicians will describe this as a perfect 12th. I can hear you ask now, why a 12th and not a 13th because 8+5=13. The reason is you take away one to make 12 because **you don't count the octave note twice.** You could also count up 12 from the bottom note, for example, The 12th note above C will be a G, but this counting up notes method is rather slow and tedious.

Here are a few examples

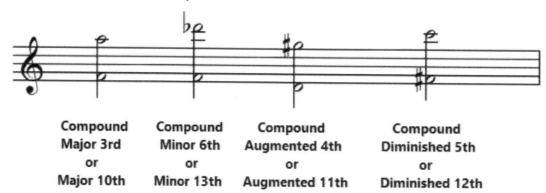

Compound	Compound	Compound	Compound
Major 3rd	Minor 6th	Augmented 4th	Diminished 5th
or	or	or	or
Major 10th	Minor 13th	Augmented 11th	Diminished 12th

All other rules from previous lessons on intervals, in levels 1-4 are the same.

Questions

Name the following intervals, being careful of the key signatures.

Lesson 5.7 - Naming Chords

Chords are identified by which degree of the scale is at their root (the base note of the chord). In a previous lesson you already came across the tonic, subdominant and dominant triads. Now you will also use chord II (Roman numerals are commonly used to describe chords and in fact are an easier way of doing so).

So for example, in E minor the chords you need are:

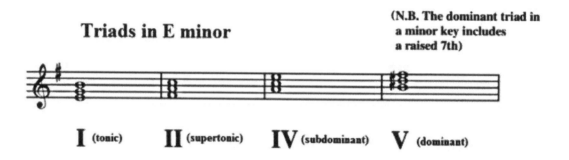

Triads in E minor

(N.B. The dominant triad in a minor key includes a raised 7th)

I (tonic)　　**II** (supertonic)　　**IV** (subdominant)　　**V** (dominant)

In addition to this, you will also need to identify which inversion of a chord is being used. There are three to chose from:

● Root position - as you see in the above examples
● 1st inversion - with the middle of the chord as its lowest note
● 2nd inversion - with the top of the chord as its lowest note.

Here are the three inversion of a tonic triad in D major

The 3 inversions of the tonic triad of D major

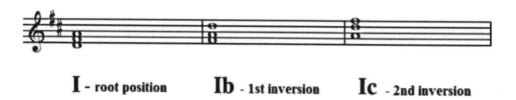

I - root position　　　**Ib** - 1st inversion　　　**Ic** - 2nd inversion

Notice how they are described with Roman numerals and then a letter after them (the first chord is really Ia but traditionally we leave off the "a").

Sounding a bit complicated? Follow these simple rules to name a chord.

1. Establish what key you are in.
2. Write out the notes in each of the triads I, II, IV, V
3. See what notes are in your chord and so decide which triad it is.
4. See which is the bottom note of your chord to decide which inversion you have.

For example, lets apply the above method to this chord. The key is A major.

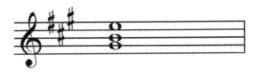

Following steps 1 - 4   above:
1. We are already given that the key is A major
2. Write out the primary triads in that key

> Chord I - A, C#, E
> Chord II - B, D, F#
> Chord IV - D, F#, A
> Chord V - E, G#, B

3. The notes in the given chord match those of chord V

4. The lowest note in the given chord is the middle note in chord V so it is in 1st inversion.

Therefore the chord is Vb

Questions

1. Name the following chords with these *major* key signatures

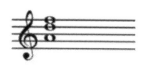

2. Name the following chords with these *minor* key signatures

Lesson 5.8 - Chords at Cadence Points

Following on from the **previous lesson** you will now learn how to choose two or three chords to fit a melody at the end of a phrase (called a cadence).

The chords you have to choose from are the same as those in the previous lesson, i.e. I, II, IV & V.

To make it easier you do not have to state at this stage which inversion of the chord you are going to use.

There are also set patterns of "chord progressions" that are used at cadence points, so if you learn these progressions you can't go wrong. In Grade 5 ABRSM Music Theory, you will only need:

V - I   (A perfect cadence)
IV - I   (A plagal cadence)
I - V   (An imperfect cadence)
II - V   (An imperfect cadence)
IV - V   (An imperfect cadence)

In Trinity Theory, the first one is covered at Grade 3, the second one at Grade 4, and the last three at Grade 5.

There may also be a third chord to choose just before the final two but this will be quite obvious as you will have already used up two of the options and you cannot put two identical chords next to each other, so that narrows down the possibilities.

So how do you decide which chords to choose?

Like you did in the previous lesson simply follow a few simple rules.

1. Decide what key you are in - these will be very basic major keys in the examination.

2. Write out (as you did the last time) the notes of the triads I, II, IV & V

3. Deal with the last two chords of a cadence first and find which chords have notes in common with the melody line. There may be more than one answer but if you remember to use the "chord progressions" above that will narrow it down. There may also be more than one melody note for each chord in which case just "harmonize" the first melody note above the chord.

4. If applicable, work out any third chord preceding the last two.

So let's try an example:

Choose chords at the places marked * to fit the melody lines at the following cadence.

Using the rules described above,
1. The key is F major.

2. Writing out the triads of I, II, IV and V in Fmajor:
   Chord I - F, A, C
   Chord II - G, B♭, D
   Chord IV - B♭, D, F
   Chord V - C, E, G

3. Dealing with the last two chords first, find a chord that has notes in common with the melody:

   The 2nd chord **could be** II **or** V although the "C" that follows seems to suggest more the latter

   The 3rd chord **could be** I **or** IV

The only possible chord progression that fits the above permutations is V to I.

4. The first chord could have been I or IV but since I has been used it is more likely to be IV.

Therefore the complete progression is **IV - V - I**

Questions

Choose suitable chords, at the places marked with an asterisk, for these two cadences to fit the melody notes given. You do not need to write out the chords, just label them as "Roman Numerals".

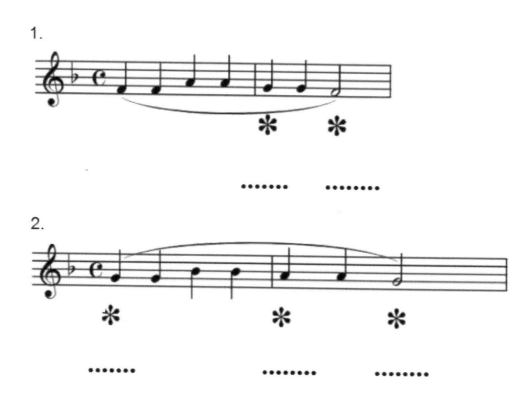

Lesson 5.9 - Musical Terms

Below is a table of terms and signs which are needed for a Grade 5 Theory Exam. Note that in ABRSM you will need to know some **German Terms** as well as Italian ones. To test yourself on these, try our FREE flashcards web app on: https://www.music-online.org.uk/p/lesson-theory-quiz-05.html

Italian Terms

attacca	go straight on
dolente	sad, mournful
dolore	grief (*doloroso*: sorrowful)
doppio movimento	twice as fast
estinto	as soft as possible, lifeless
incalzando	getting quicker
lacrimoso	sad
loco	at the normal pitch
lunga	long
lusingando	coaxing,
misura	measure
ossia	or, alternatively
piacevole	pleasant
piangevole	plaintive,
pochettino, poch.	rather little
rinforzando, rf, rfz	reinforcing
segue	go straight on
smorzando, smorz.	dying away in tone and speed
teneramente, tenerezza	tenderly, tenderness
tosto	swift, rapid
volante	flying fast

German Terms

aber	but
ausdruck	expression
bewegt	with movement, agitated
breit	broad, expansive
ein	a, one
einfach	simple
etwas	somewhat, rather
fröhlich	cheerful, joyful
immer	always
langsam	slow
lebhaft	lively
mässig	at a moderate speed
mit	with
nicht	not
ohne	without
ruhig	peaceful
schnell	fast
sehr	very
süss	sweet
traurig	sad
und	and
voll	full
wenig	little
wieder	again
zart	tender, delicate
zu	to, too

<u>ANSWERS</u>

Lesson 1.1 - Answers

1.

2.

3. Three crotchet beats in a bar.

4. A minim is worth the same as 8 semiquavers

5. Common Time.

Lesson 1.2 - Answers

1.

2.

3.

A - The stem should go *up on the right*.
B - The note head is not centred on the line, it's more below than above
C - The stem should go down *on the left.*
D - The curly tail should be on the right

Lesson 1.3 - Answers

1.

2.

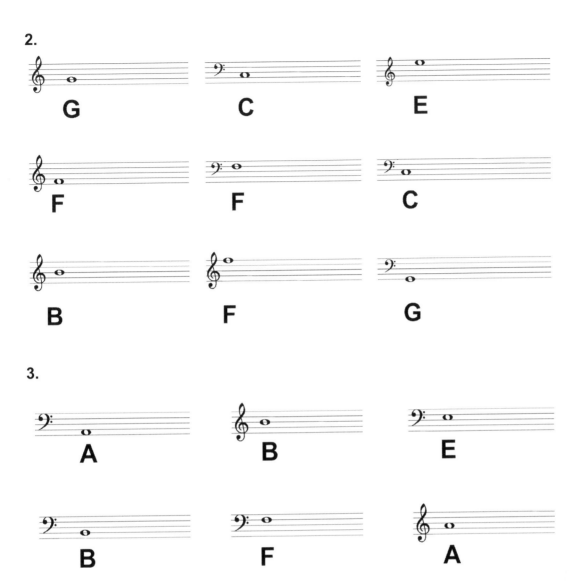

G C E

F F C

B F G

3.

A B E

B F A

Lesson 1.4 - Answers

Lesson 1.5 - Answers
1.

Quaver   crotchet   minim   semiquaver

2.

Lesson 1.6 - Answers

1.

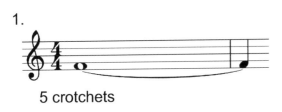

5 crotchets

2.

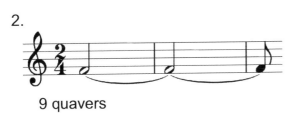

9 quavers

3 & 4.

Lesson 1.7 - Answers

Lesson 1.8 - Answers

1.

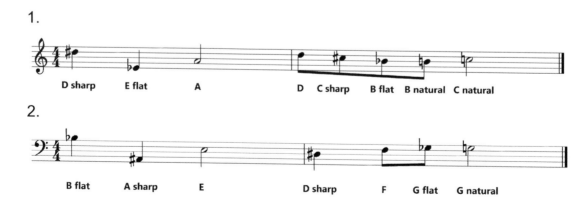

3.

4.

5.

Lesson 1.9 - Answers

1.

Key **D major**

Key **G major**

Key **F major**

2.

G major

C major

D major

D major

F major

C major

Lesson 1.10 Answers

1.

7th

3rd

8th/8ve

4th

5th

6th

2.

5th   7th   1st/8th   6th   3rd   1st   4th   2nd   5th

3.

6th

3rd

8th/8ve

4th

2nd

5th

Lesson 1.11 Answers
1.

C major

D major

C major

F major

G major

F major

2.

Lesson 2.1 Answers

1

C A G B B C

2.

D D C E E F

3.

4.

Lesson 2.2 Answers

1.
a) 3 crotchet beats in a bar
b) 2 minim beats in a bar
c) 3 quaver beats in a bar

2.

. 3.

Lesson 2.3 Answers

1. D major, F major, E flat major

2.

3.

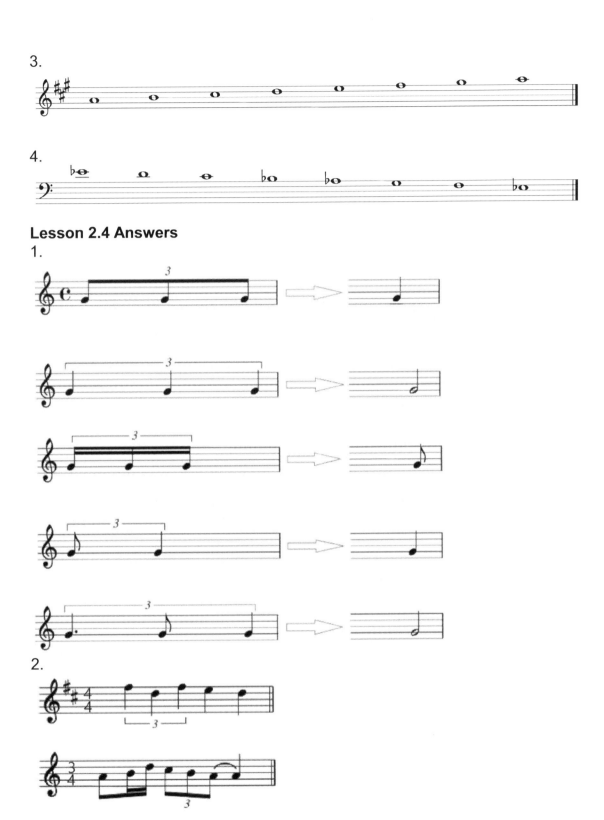

4.

Lesson 2.4 Answers

1.

2.

Lesson 2.5 Answers

1. A minor, E minor

2.

E minor   D minor

3.
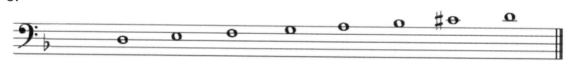

4.

Lesson 2.6 Answers

1.

2.

3.

Lesson 2.7 Answers

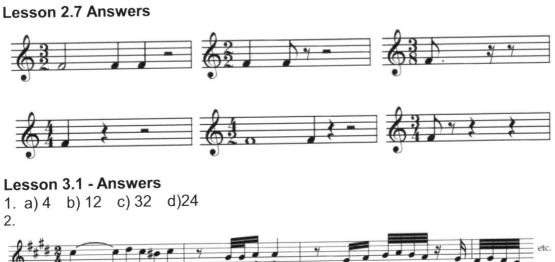

Lesson 3.1 - Answers

1. a) 4   b) 12   c) 32   d)24

2.

3

4.

Lesson 3.2 - Answers

1.

2.

3.

4.

Lesson 3.3 - Answers

1.

D sharp	A flat	G sharp
B sharp	E flat	F
E flat	A sharp	C
G sharp	B flat	E flat

2.

Lesson 3.4 - Answers

1.

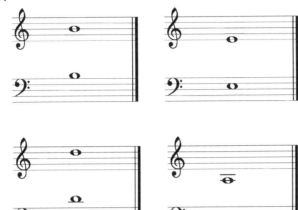

2.

3.

Lesson 3.5 - Answers

1. 9/8 time

2.

3.

4.

Lesson 3.6 - Answers

1. C harmonic minor

2.

3.

C minor   C# minor

4.

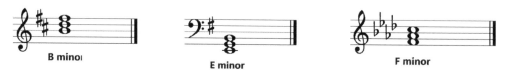

B minor   E minor   F minor

Lesson 3.7 - Answers

1. Major 7th, Perfect 4th, Perfect 5th, Minor 3rd

2.

Lesson 3.8 - Answers

1.

2.

Lesson 4.1 - Answers

1.& 2.

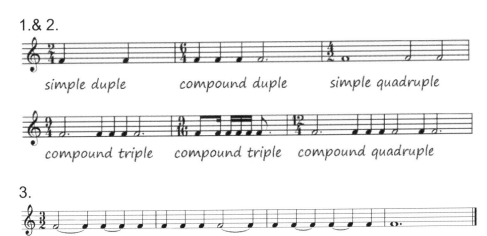

simple duple   compound duple   simple quadruple

compound triple   compound triple   compound quadruple

3.

Lesson 4.2 - Answers

1. a) 4   b) 16   c) 64

2.

Lesson 4.3 - Answers

1.   **2.**

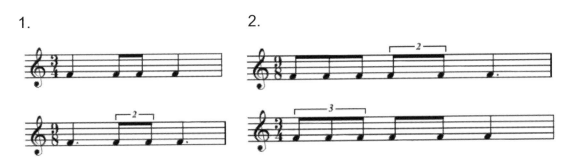

3. When converting from simple time to compound time we add duplets and dots and lose triplets.

4. When converting from compound time to simple time we add triplets and lose duplets and dots.

Lesson 4.4 - Answers

1.

G E C G A D F D

2.

3.

Lesson 4.5 - Answers

1. "G double sharp, is an enharmonic equivalent of A and B double flat.

2.

Lesson 4.6 - Answers

1.

E major   E flat major   B major   A flat major

2.

3.

E harmonic minor ascending

B flat melodic minor ascending

F sharp melodic minor descending

G sharp harmonic minor descending

Lesson 4.7 - Answers

1.

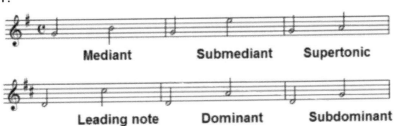

| Mediant | Submediant | Supertonic |

| Leading note | Dominant | Subdominant |

2.

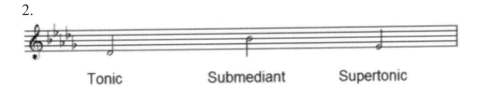

| Tonic | Submediant | Supertonic |

Lesson 4.8 - Answers

1.

2.

N.B. This is only one of various possible answers

Lesson 4.9 - Answers

Perfect 5th	Minor 3rd	Diminished 7th	Augmented 2nd
Perfect 4th	Minor 6th	Diminished Octave	Augmented 3rd
Augmented 2nd	Diminished 5th	Augmented 4th	Diminished 6th

Lesson 4.10 - Answers

1.

Dominant   Tonic   Subdominant

.

2.

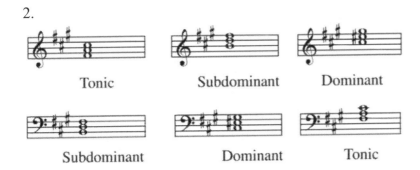

Tonic   Subdominant   Dominant

Subdominant   Dominant   Tonic

Lesson 4.11 - Answers

1.

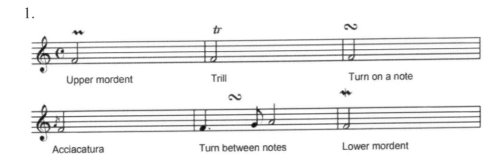

Upper mordent   Trill   Turn on a note

Acciacatura   Turn between notes   Lower mordent

2.

Acciaccatura   Turn on a note   Upper mordent

Lower mordent   Turn between notes   Trill

Lesson 4.12 - Answers

1. Tuba or Trombone

2. Pizzicato - meaning to pluck the string

3. Viola

4. The use of a) the alto clef and b) up bow and down bow markings

Lesson 5.1 - Answers

1.

2.

Lesson 5.2 - Answers

1.

2.

3.

Lesson 5.3 - Answers

1.

2.

3.

Lesson 5.4 - Answers

1.

F sharp major/
D sharp minor

D major/
B minor

G major/
E minor

G flat major/
E flat minor

2.

Lesson 5.5 - Answers

Lesson 5.6 - Answers

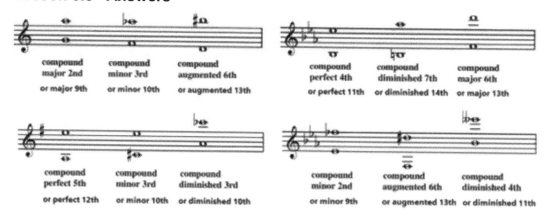

Lesson 5.7 - Answers

1.

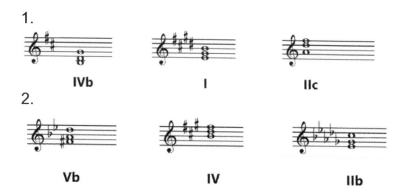

IVb   **I**   **IIc**

2.

Vb   **IV**   **IIb**

Lesson 5.8 - Answers

1. V-I   2. II-I-V

Printed in Great Britain
by Amazon

46138550R00099